THE **100** GREATEST SALES IDEAS OF ALL TIME

THE 100
GREATEST SALES
IDEAS OF ALL TIME

KEN LANGDON

CAPSTONE

Copyright © Ken Langdon 2003

The right of Ken Langdon to be identified as the author of this book has been asserted in accordance with the Copyright, Designs and Patents Act 1988

First Published 2003 by
Capstone Publishing Limited (a Wiley company)
The Atrium
Southern Gate
Chichester PO19 8SQ
http://www.wileyeurope.com

CIP catalogue records for this book are available from the British Library and the US Library of Congress

ISBN 1-84112-141-X

Typeset in 11/14pt Plantin by Sparks Computer Solutions Ltd, Oxford, UK
http://www.sparks.co.uk

Printed and bound by T.J. International Ltd, Padstow, Cornwall

Substantial discounts on bulk quantities of Capstone Books are available to corporations, professional associations and other organizations. For details telephone Capstone Publishing on (+44-1865-798623), fax (+44-1865-240941) or email (info@wiley-capstone.co.uk)

Contents

The Top Two Greatest Sales Ideas of All Time and Five that Make Them Useable, Plus the Start to Selling Value   1

The Ten Greatest Sales Ideas for Creating Interest   15

The Ten Greatest Sales Ideas for Establishing Need · 27

The Seven Greatest Sales Ideas for Selling Through an Agreed Basis of Decision · 35

The Eight Greatest Sales Ideas for Presenting Your Case   **45**

The Five Greatest Sales Ideas for Remembering that There is Always a Way   **59**

The Four Greatest Sales Ideas for Selling in a Small Retail Outlet

The Six Greatest Sales Ideas for Dealing with Difficult Products and Markets

The Seven Greatest Sales Tips for Salespeople

The Six Greatest Sales Ideas for Planning a Complex Sale 81

The Four Greatest Sales Ideas for Qualifying Out Proactively 95

The Three Greatest Sales Ideas for Closing the Deal Softly, Softly 99

The Ten Greatest Ideas for Implementing Account Management 103

The Ten Greatest Sales Tips for Sales Managers 119

*B*ackground

This is a book for anyone who in their business life has to do some selling – and that means everyone in business. It will help people who have to sell ideas or actions to their seniors and subordinates as much as it will help professional full-time salespeople. In all cases it will improve your technique and attitude and, most importantly, it will improve your sales performance; that is, you will be more successful in getting people to agree with your position and carry out the actions you prefer, whether getting a promotion or getting the order. Not only that, but it will also improve your ability to bring up your kids and get your own way in family and social settings as well.

To show you how I can make such a huge claim I need to explain the background. Here is a very good bit of solution selling.

Four years ago a major book retailer was planning a summer campaign to sell business books at airports and railway stations. The marketing strategy behind the campaign was to attract business people to take a business book on holiday with them. The account manager, some would call him the salesman for the account, of a publisher who had an excellent relationship with his client came up with the idea of using a new book as a front to attract people into the business section. The retailer liked it and agreed that they wanted a book that was not too serious but nevertheless plainly a business book from which people could learn.

The publisher came up with all the main ingredients that the publishing industry finds important in a book project – nothing to do with the contents, of course, but all to do with the design. It was to be a 7x7 inch book so that it fitted on the end shelves in the bookshops facing you as you come in the door. It was to have a fairly large font so that it looked like an easy read and was to have a lot of white space on the page for the same reason. The cover design had to bear in mind that if the book went well it might be the start of a short series. This meant that it had to have an area on the cover that could, by changing the colour, signal another book in the same series. Because it was 7x7 and in a big font they knew how many words would be in the book, around 50,000, therefore what its cost would be and therefore what price they could charge – a straight tenner. Not nine pounds 99 but a clean deal at the checkout it's yours for ten pounds, one note.

At this point they had a project with one major deficiency – yes, you have probably guessed it; they needed a title. Those of you who guessed that the one deficiency was an author or actual copy have plainly not spent much time in the publishing business, particularly the pop end of non-fiction. The publisher came up with the title because, after all, that is their business. It was to be called *The 100 Greatest Business Ideas of All Time*.

Middle management then had to sell the idea to top management because the investment in this case was real, not virtual as it is with most books. The deal was that the retailer would have exclusive rights to sell the first print run of the book, and the next two in the series, but without their normal deal of sale or return. If it did not sell, it stayed in their warehouse; it did not go back to the publisher's. A manager drove the project through the return on investment process that the company uses, and after some time and a few glitches the budget was agreed and the project given the go-ahead. There was now seven weeks to go before the book had to be on the shelves.

I tell this story at the start of a book on great sales ideas for two reasons. Firstly because it illustrates, I think, very well what client care and solution selling is fundamentally about. It is an obvious point, I know, but it raises some quite interesting issues of technique. If you are going to care for your client, and by so doing sell them lots of your products and services, you must spend time and energy understanding their real needs – not their perceived needs, although you must understand those as well, but their real needs. Satisfying these is actually how you maintain a long-term mutually beneficial relationship with clients. And it is difficult. It is difficult first and foremost because there are two types of need involved here – the things the organisation needs to do in order to meet its objectives, and the things that managers need in order to advance their careers or give them an easy life or whatever turns them on. In the case of this book, the needs neatly coincided. The organisation needed a book that would attract people into the business section, looked readable as a holiday book but could still be put on expenses. Middle managers were looking for an innovative bit of creative thinking that would make sure that they would sell more business books that summer.

The publisher was laughing all the way to the bank, since it is not often that they get a guaranteed sure-fire winner, and the book retailer was busy rewarding and promoting the three or four people who claimed, modestly, to be responsible for the innovative idea. Meanwhile, the publisher's project manager knew they had to get a book out, and in order to get a book out they needed an author and that was where I came in. He phoned me: would I write *The 100 Greatest Business Ideas of All Time* – in four weeks. Well I wasn't sure, it looked like hard work to be honest and I would have to change one or two things on my schedule. But my agent and my business partner thought that the money was right, so, well, I made the decision to do it.

So I sat down to write. The 100 Greatest Business Ideas of All Time – 1 – hmmm – ... war, yes, that had to be one of the best. War is very good for business. You can make a load of money building the weapons and ammunition that destroy buildings and then make a load more money putting the buildings back up after the war. OK, that's definitely one of the best business ideas around. 2. Religion, yes, that's a good one. Religion probably has few equals in giving rise to thousands of business opportunities. From the Egyptian temples and pyramids, to the worldwide chain of mosques and churches, religion has given work to architects, builders, painters, icon manufacturers, musicians and every other trade and profession you can think of.

At this point I ran out of ideas. So, 98 ideas short and half a day less than four weeks to go, I shouted for help. I e-mailed everyone in my address book and got the publisher to do the same. I was then awash with excellent ideas from colleagues and fellow writers for me to follow up and use. That technique worked a treat and it became a good read and was very successful. When I came earlier this year to write the next in the series, I shouted for help right at the start of the project, which was to write a book entitled *The 100 Greatest Sales Ideas of All Time*.

So, there is the picture. Because I have been a salesman all my life, most of the people in my address book are or have been in the sales function. I was simply asking for their best tips and those techniques that they had discovered work for them. I also wrote to the Chairmen of half of the FTSE-100 and an astonishing number of them replied or passed my letter to their sales directors or HR people.

In my opinion those ideas that they thought most important must hold real clues as to how a professional account manager should behave, and it is those ideas that make up the majority of this book. Some of the people who gave ideas are professional business people who have learnt how to be persuasive from their experience and by watching others. Some are professional salespeople who are trained and retrained in the latest techniques and methodologies for making sales, particularly solution-oriented selling, where they use their products and services to solve customer problems of which they are aware. Many are, like myself, sales training consultants working on the organisation of sales forces as well as on various elements of training salespeople from rookies to seasoned account managers. I cannot count all the ideas they have come up with and it has been a great task to refine them into this book.

*I*ntroduction

I have been selling for all my business life. It is interesting to note that anyone who has been in business could make the same claim. It is not possible to survive in any commercial activity unless you sell your products or services. What is a career-minded person doing as they take on projects outside their normal job in order to impress their superiors and gain better access to senior people in their organisation? They are selling their services as suitable for promotion. What is a jobbing carpenter doing when they produce heart-shaped wooden boxes for Valentine's Day and offer them to clients they have worked for in the past? They are selling the boxes and also just reminding their customers of their existence and their ability to provide further services. What is a bank manager doing when they agree to make a speech at their old school? And I could go on.

'Everybody lives by selling something' is a phrase coined not by a red-necked republican in the oil industry but by the aesthete Robert Louis Stevenson, the novelist and poet.

So why is my statement that I have been selling for all my business life different from any person enjoying success in their jobs, whether working for big corporations or, at the other end of the spectrum, for themselves? The answer is that my selling has been of products and services that I understood only vaguely. I knew what they would do for my customers but I was not entirely sure how or why they produced those beneficial effects. For example, for many years I sold computer systems. Now, years ago I had a passing knowledge of how computers work and of the products that I sold, but it was no more than a passing knowledge. Then they got more complicated and I had to understand the telecommunications industry as well. The list of products was so vast that I could not, with the best will in the world, maintain even this superficial knowledge. I was completely dependent on technical support people to turn my interpretation of a customer's problem into a technical solution and, if I made the sale, to implement what I had promised. And I did not have the best will in the world. By this time I was becoming a reasonable general manager with a growing knowledge of how to run a business and absolutely no interest in computers themselves.

'So what,' I hear you cry. Well, I think that this lack of real knowledge of the products and services I sell is a huge advantage in selling. It gives the professional salesperson who does nothing except sell, an edge over people who have selling as an extra skill they need to add to their real expertise. Professional salesmen have nothing else to concentrate on than improving their technique and their selling performance. Their minds are not cluttered up with expertise and technical knowledge. I have talked, for example, to chartered surveyors, people who have to have a detailed knowledge of the property market and of landlord/tenant laws, to give just two issues that they have to keep their knowledge of up-to-date. When customers ask them questions, they think through the answers right down to the level of detail they need to consider to satisfy themselves that what they are saying is accurate as well as attractive in sales terms. Professional salespeople, on the other hand, answer client questions only with the next sale in mind. That is not to say that they will be cavalier or dishonest, I am talking about professional salespeople, but it is to say that their response is aimed at moving the sale forward. If that means admitting ignorance, they will do that happily. If it means ducking the question to another day they will do that too.

The first section in the book describes the ideas that came out top for producing sustained and successful selling in my straw poll. They are not, of course, rocket science but they are the pillars on which other more refined selling techniques hinge.

Contributors

I am very grateful to the following people who came up with the tips, techniques and stories that made up the bulk of this book.

Alan Bonham, Andy Bruce, Bill Halbert, Dave Taylor, Graham Mackenzie-Washington, John Furniss, John Priestley, Kate Langdon, Nick Wenman, Nigel Lanch, Norman Strangemore, Malcolm Felgate, Mark Allin and Richard Humphreys.

The Top Two Greatest Sales Ideas of All Time and Five that Make Them Useable, Plus the Start to Selling Value

Introduction

My claim to have discovered the top two ideas comes from their popularity with the people who sent in contributions to this book. They are very interesting – the first is 'Listening', which may surprise some people who express the view that a born salesperson is one with the gift of the gab, the ability to talk Eskimos into buying fridges or rabbis into buying pork chops. But the strongly expressed view of many people is the opposite of this.

The second idea concerns being very focused on achieving quantifiable objectives at every stage of a sales campaign. You must know exactly where you want to be at the end of a sales call or at a particular date in a long tender exercise. It is that focus that distinguishes the competent businessperson from the competent businessperson with the added touch of sales awareness.

Idea 1 – Never interrupt a customer to make a point

The top idea was top by a country mile. A huge percentage of the replies made reference to it either by example or by using the actual word. The skill they spoke about most was **listening**. Active listening some of them called it.

Here is the art of listening going wrong for an architect. He had the job of advising two new homeowners on how they should use the space and carry out the refurbishment of an old run-down property they had just bought. Unfortunately there was a hiatus between the carrying out by the architect of the survey and the first meeting with the new owners. He used the time to speculate on what they might want to do with the house. What did it lack, in his view, and what would they have to do to put that lack right?

When the owners arrived for the first meeting they had prepared a list of their requirements for the property. Despite this the architect went ahead and presented the ideas that he had already sketched. After all, that is human nature. We all want to show our original ideas off since they feel so right to us. The architect was in fact interrupting the customer to make a point. When the customer eventually tabled the list, it was very different from the first thoughts of their adviser. They now had a situation of the customer not wanting to make the adviser feel bad, and the adviser feeling the need to defend his work. Despite all that went after, the relationship never got over this appalling start.

In any aspect of sales technique – including listening – I am not really comfortable with the art of selling being allied to the art of war. After all, it cannot be right to have the customer play the role of the enemy; clearly the enemy is the competition. On the other hand there is an element of struggle about it. The customer is trying to probe the salesperson's defences of integrity and truth to discover inaccuracies. The customer, with the best will in the world, recognizes that the salesperson has another agenda apart from helping the customer to solve problems or be happier. They are there to take orders of the right products (from their point of view) at the right time (also from their point of view).

Consider, too, the change in the relationship between a salesperson and a customer when the sales campaign is over and the salesperson has the order. Before the order the relationship is mutually interesting and the salesperson is working hard to engage the customer's liking and respect. After the order the important thing becomes the salesperson's company performing to specification. Now that can become a battle and the customers know it at the time of the order. As one of the contributors put it, 'The relationship is never the same after the first successful sale by a salesperson to a new customer.'

Customers can be forgiven for feeling a little like landed fish. So maybe war analogies do have some merit. Here is a version of the listening idea from a man writing about war.

> *If you know the enemy and know yourself, you need not fear the result of a hundred battles. If you know yourself but not the enemy, for every victory gained you will also suffer a defeat. If you know neither the enemy nor yourself, you will succumb in every battle.*
>
> Sun Tzu, *The Art of War*

To get to know yourself and your enemy takes the art of listening, the top sales idea of all time.

Idea 2 – Focus on milestones and progress targets

The next thing that a lot of senior people came up with concerned the objectives of meetings. Fundamentally, most business people do too little in terms of preparing the exact objectives of a meeting with a client. I formed a team with an excellent salesman and we sold sales training into large companies. He was the account manager and, of course, if we got the business, I did the training. The way we planned calls was very detailed. We actually sketched out precisely the one or two sentences or phrases we wanted the client to say at the end of the call. This gave us terrific focus for the call. It also gave us a lot of merriment. If the people actually used the words it was quite hard to keep a straight face.

A lot of managing directors and Chairmen talked about focus in meetings. Partly, perhaps, because their diaries tend to be a series of relatively short meetings and they want people to get to the point, and partly – this is back to my theory of the specialist salesperson being uncluttered by expertise – because the people at the top of an organisation tend to have become general managers rather than experts.

Sales trainers spend a lot of their training time in role-play. They play the customer while the salespeople simply set about doing their job as sales-people. The biggest single frustration with doing the job of the customer in a role-play is the feeling that someone has just popped in for a chat. In the debrief at the end of the meeting the salesperson would say that they thought the call had gone pretty well; whilst the customer had no problem with the call, just an empty feeling that they had wasted their time. The cure for this is to have a single-minded focus on a sales objective and the use of good closing technique to find out if you have achieved the objective or at least whether you are on the way. So the next three great sales ideas are the essential techniques involved in doing this.

There are many ways of trying to remember this focus and to use closing questions, but I have found these three to be the best of them – ABC, STEP and SMART.

Idea 3 – ABC: Always Be Closing

We do not know who first coined this phrase, but it's spot on. Everyone has to ginger up their communication skills by practising and using good closing and trial closing technique. This is true not only when you are actually trying to reach an objective such as getting the order, it is also useful when trying to measure the progress you are making in any form of communication – on the telephone, in a sales call or at any meeting.

ABC – Always be closing

- Salesman: 'Which of the colours fits best with your kitchen decoration the grey or the light blue?' (This is called an alternative close.)
- Manager: 'If you had those resources would you take responsibility for achieving that objective?' (Trial close)
- Mother: 'If you had your own clothing allowance would you keep your room tidy' (Associated project close)
- Teenager: 'But everyone's getting them, so if you don't buy me them now there will be none left.' (Impending event close)

This technique could equally be called 'Don't duck the issue'. Sometimes we fail to ask a closing question because we are scared of a negative response, or because we know that the customer is going to say no because they are simply not in a position yet to say yes. Maybe we are bored or the time is running short and we realise that we will have to come back for another go. Whatever it is, don't make the mistake of failing to check where you have got to in the eyes of the customer. After all, if a customer says that they are not convinced that they need a particular feature of your product you can always ask why or use the stock 'What would I have to do to convince you of this point' to make further progress.

The other technique that makes for focused selling is allied to ABC; it is STEP.

Idea 4 – STEP: Signal The End Point

If you have to persuade someone to change their minds or move from a neutral position on a decision to a positive one, it is also easy to duck the issue at the beginning of whatever persuasive activity you are engaged in. Using the medium of a presentation, let us look at this.

You are trying to get agreement from your board to put two new people into your team over six months to take charge of arranging trade shows. Prior to this, the trade shows had somehow happened, but with a lot of last minute panic and favours being asked of various people within and without the company. These last minute panics tend to cost a lot of money, as the alternative of not being ready for opening day is unacceptable. (How much does an electrician charge per hour when it is 6 o'clock in the evening before the show opens and your stand has at present only a temporary spotlight?) The general professionalism of your exhibits is also, you are convinced, inferior to the other companies at the show.

The board is likely to be sceptical since this is new expenditure with no exceptional new results.

From what has gone before in this section you have prepared your closing question. 'Do I have your agreement to go out to the usual recruitment agency and instruct them to hire two grade 4's straight away?' It's nice and specific with no room for ambiguity or subsequent backsliding.

Now think about your opening. A lot of people would fudge the opening, preferring to launch into horror stories of what has happened in the past, showing the board a list of extra shows which you could put on if you had the resources and so on. This tends to put the board on its guard. Remember, very few managers go to the board with any suggestion that does not require additional resources and it is frustrating when they do not have a clue about how much you are going to ask for.

Much better is to signal the closing question right at the beginning of the presentation. It goes something like this:

'You have given me ten minutes so I'll get to the point as quickly as possible. I am going to cover three topics in the ten minutes. First I am going to go over the current situation we face in arranging and setting up exhibition stands, then I am going to ask your permission to hire two extra grade 4 people to carry out that role in the future, and with any time that is left I'll show you our current ideas for the next big show. Is that OK?'

The insertion of the closed question at the end of this statement can be very revealing. It can lead to a huge row. 'No you bloody well cannot have more people, these shows are more trouble than they are worth already' and so on. At least you are arguing about the point you are trying to make. More often you will get a neutral reply such as 'Yes, OK, but if we have any problems with the first bit, we will not be agreeing to the second bit.' Incidentally, if this remark comes from the most senior person in the room it will generally get a laugh, which is always good. Sometimes you will get a more positive response and you will wonder why you are making the presentation at all.

Whatever happens you will have made real progress towards getting a decision and your own way. The message is clear – be upfront about what you are going to ask for by grasping the nettle and taking the STEP at an early stage.

Idea 5 – SMART: Stretching, Measurable, Achievable, Related to the customer and Time-targeted

Let's move up just a bit from the focus of a meeting and closing for milestones, and think about the art of setting objectives. I am old enough to remember when setting Objectives and the Key Tasks necessary to achieve the objectives was a fairly new concept at the individual level. Nowadays no one in their right mind would take on a job where the objectives were not specific and agreed between the two parties: the manager and the person with the objective to achieve.

And yet it is surprising how poor the quality of these objectives frequently is. They simply do not live up to the essential attributes of a good objective. Let's take a team that is working together and work out how they can be sure that their objectives are consistent and that the sum of all the objectives will reach the overall objective the team is tackling. The trick is to make them SMART. Once again, I am not sure who first coined this acronym. To be honest, I thought it was me for a long time, but the term appears so frequently in books and training manuals that I am now not sure.

Incidentally, I took the phrase into common parlance in Hewlett Packard when I ran a series of training courses for their salespeople. Years later the word SMART was still in use, but I was amazed that only one word was the same as I had used in the original training courses. Talk about Chinese whispers and 'Send re-enforcements we are about to advance' becoming 'Send three and fourpence we are going to a dance'.

Anyway, here is my version of this immensely useful acronym.

To be an acceptable statement of a team's aim, a goal in any plan must be SMART:

- **S**tretching
- **M**easurable
- **A**chievable
- **R**elated to the customer
- **T**ime-targeted

Stretching

There is no point in wasting precious time on planning an objective that is going to occur even if the team went off on a cycling tour of the Scottish Highlands. The job has to be difficult enough to merit the time required to make and implement the plan.

Further, it is the role of the salesperson to change the world. He or she needs to set goals which test the ability of the team to be persuasive, i.e. to change people's behaviour. A good planning session will often change or add to the original goal as the team examines what the opportunities are.

If this happens it is indeed right to change the goal. With all elements of any plan, you need to remain flexible to an ever-changing environment and to new ideas.

Measurable

The normal measure of a sales goal is a sum of money that the team is going to achieve in revenues or in profits.

In theory the team should be interested in both, and set a target that predicts the revenue value and the resultant profit. In practice many companies, for good reasons, do not give the profit responsibility to salespeople at all and they may even not be able to predict profitability.

Other measures in a sales campaign can be more qualitative than quantitative. You may set an objective to impress someone with a demonstration, for example, but in most cases you can get even these measures down to a number. 'On a scale of one to ten, how did you find the demonstrated performance of this equipment?'

It is unfortunate when team leaders see an opportunity, prove a good business case and then fail to agree the goal because people are not willing to propose the risk to senior management.

Achievable

Having made certain that the goal is stretching, the team must also believe that it can be achieved. The team should be sufficiently close to the problem or opportunity to recognize where there is a feasible chance of success.

The achievability test is particularly important where new technology is being considered that managers will recognize as carrying extra risk. It is unfortunate when team leaders see an opportunity, prove a good business case and then fail to agree the goal because people are not willing to propose the risk to senior management.

The key to checking achievability is to ask this question of as many people as possible and at as high a level as possible: 'Do you think this team can achieve this objective in the current circumstances?'

Related to the customer

Just as we must be able to see what the benefit of the objective is for the team in terms of revenues and profits, so we must also get a flavour of what is in it for their customer. Be the customer internal or external, this rule still applies. If they are setting objectives that do not have a benefit to their customer, they have to ask themselves why.

The action of checking the objective with the customer can be useful in terms of getting the customer's agreement on the main benefit statement that the team will aim at while implementing the plan. Incidentally, this book uses the word 'customer' to include external and internal customers; so if your selling or persuasiveness is all aimed at people inside your organisation, they are your customers.

Time-targeted

The date of the completion of the goal completes the rules of setting appropriate objectives.

It is uncanny how many objectives are targeted to end by the date of the completion of the company's financial year. Once again, the concentration must be on the customer's view. Is the timescale suitable for him as well for the team?

Idea 6 – Listen to and learn from other people's jargon

As a salesperson working to understand your customer as well as you know yourself, you are *ipso facto* going to be skating on thin ice from time to time, when discussing the other person's job and expertise. Have confidence. Most people are happy to explain what they do and the words they use. Besides which, a little bit of bluffing can, at fairly low risk, pay handsomely in terms of pleasing people by sounding as though you understand what they do. It is a question of taking careful notes, reworking their words and repeating the ideas back.

Here is an example from the publishing business. A commissioning editor was in full selling mode as he tried to get a Nobel Prize winner to write a book for his publishing company. The scientist says, 'I could be interested in doing something on my work on the electromagnetic properties of wood, given the new work published recently by Professor X.' 'So,' says the salesman, repeating the jargon with slight changes, 'You are studying in the same area of research as Professor X, who I guess has made a major contribution to the field of electromagnetism.' 'You know my work?' says astonished and impressed Nobel Prize winner.

Take care not to affect too much knowledge that you do not have in this area, but risk and return go hand in hand and no salesperson made target without taking some risks.

Idea 7 – Understanding the real need

OK, so getting people to talk about themselves their jobs and their problems is generally not too difficult.

(Just as an aside to that, and to balance this, I must report on a meeting, one of the most uncomfortable I have ever attended, with a senior person who came to the meeting because her boss had told her that my software product had potential for applications within their organisation. Have you ever seen anyone absolutely determined to be unimpressed by a product? My open questions about her major issues were met with a blank refusal to discuss them with me. I finished the demo and came out resolving yet again never to go into a meeting to demonstrate a product unless I knew something of the real needs and issues of the other person. I still make this mistake after all these years.)

Finding the real need is a question of further thought and probing. Your product or service is there to solve a problem for the customer or to allow them to exploit an opportunity. Sometimes the solution may be part of something bigger that is more difficult to describe. Here is an example of a team of managers misunderstanding the fundamental strategy of their own business, let alone someone else's.

Sometimes the solution may be part of something bigger that is more difficult to describe.

The CEO of Parker pens who was in post while the company was having a bad time, asked his senior team who their competition were. They replied, as you would expect, with Waterman, Bic, Biro and so forth. 'No,' says the CEO, 'Here is our competition,' and produced a Dunhill lighter. 'We are not in the pens business any more,' he said, 'We are in the executive gifts business.'

The next complication to understanding real needs in business-to-business selling is, as we have said, that you have to divide the needs into two types – institutional and personal. In fact, it is a very good sales technique to draw this up as a matrix, with the organisation's needs across the top and the personal needs of the key people down the side. Then look for places where they might coincide. Where there is a tick you find your most straightforward opportunities, where there is a cross or mismatch you know the areas where you have, in one way or another, got to work hard and change something. Doing this also helps with demonstrating how a service you are selling not only solves a client problem and gives a good return on investment, but also supports the overall strategy of the organisation as explained to you by the high level board room contacts which you should have.

One other example of this – I was selling a training programme to help a company to get its sales force to emphasize in their sales proposals the customer's business problems rather than the merits of their products and services. They plainly needed it. Senior customer managers were ignoring the salespeople and their proposals and the hit rate of proposals tendered to orders received was going down. The person who was responsible for sales development programmes was an ambitious man who had not been in the job long. It was plain that he wanted my solution but equally clear that he had some reluctance to go ahead with my proposal as it stood. I suddenly realised the real personal need. He wanted to kick-start his reputation in the new job by appearing in front of a lot of salespeople and sales managers early on and impressing them with a new idea for a process that would obviously increase sales. My programme offered this, but he felt it was rather lame for him to appear as the owner of the idea but not its implementer. That is, he felt it unsatisfactory that I would be the obvious front man in the training.

I changed my proposal, selling him the system and a 'train the trainer' event for him so that he could go round the sales force doing the actual training. Organisational need and personal need were now in sync and he went ahead.

Idea 8 – Remember that nobody said life was easy

Let us finish this first section of the top two sales ideas and the five techniques that make them implementable by reminding ourselves that although we may as sales-people have the occasional 'bluebird', the order that comes in without our putting any or much effort into getting it, mostly it takes hard graft.

A sales manager contributor said this:

> *Sometimes selling takes not only focus but also hard work. I remember a salesman in London selling accounting systems. Every Friday we used to go to the pub at lunchtime to celebrate deals won or drown our sorrows. This man didn't turn up one Friday and everybody assumed he had had a bad week. Later that afternoon he arrived back at the office with a handful of orders he had closed that morning. He had decided to do a few hours' cold calling as he was in an area he hadn't done much prospecting in before and that was why he had missed the gathering.*

Idea 9 – Start thinking about selling value

Apart from making contacts – that is, getting people to whom you can sell – the most difficult thing that salespeople have to handle is differentiation: why should customers buy from you rather than anyone else and how do you prove that the price being asked is fair? Both of these questions boil down to a common theme uniting a number of great ideas, all united round the subject of selling value.

Here is a simple definition of value – the market value of a product is what the market is willing to pay for it the next time a sale is made. How much, for example, is your house worth? You can hazard a fairly reliable guess by looking at what a similar house went for recently; but you will never really know unless you accept an offer from someone to buy it. At that point you know exactly the market value of your house. The following day its market value could be more or less, and so it goes on.

Here is the value concept being coached into a new assistant by an old and wily optician. He explains that when the customer asks how much the new glasses will be, you tell them the price: 'Fifty pounds.' If they don't wince, you say, 'Per lens.' If they still don't wince, you add, 'Plus the frames.'

Conclusion

This is the only section of the book that is, in my view, in numerical order. It has the top two ideas as stated by the many contributors of material and ideas, and it has the basic selling or persuading techniques you need to implement them. Now we move on to other great ideas, but not necessarily in order. Rather, they form a reference book of ideas you may dip into from time to time. For the sake of some structure I have put them into sections that roughly correspond to the steps you go through in a professional sales campaign:

ABC – Always be closing

Incidentally, you are not still browsing are you? If so, isn't it time you made a decision to go ahead, take this book to the checkout and pay for it?

The Ten Greatest Sales Ideas for Creating Interest

Introduction

Before you can sell anything, face to face, over the telephone or off the page, you have to engage their interest. Many salespeople get this very early stage wrong. Marketing resources are, by their function, better at this but often make the mistake of misunderstanding how the sale will be taken forward after interest has been shown. This leads to salespeople fighting against rather than with their sales collateral, advertising, brochures sponsorships or whatever. Nowhere does the co-ordination of the two functions need to be better co-ordinated than at the stage of attracting the prospect's interest.

It is difficult, for example, for a salesperson not to appear to be going through a routine that has been tried and tested by other salespeople that prospects have met. Does anyone, for example, believe a doorstep person who starts off by saying 'Don't worry, I have not come to sell you anything'? There is a pattern to selling, whether it is face to face or telephone selling that people recognize. We would do well to break the mould and interest people by using techniques they have not seen before, particularly in opening a presentation, a conversation or a proposal. Openings are so important that a professional salesperson prepares the actual words they will use as part of the preparation for a sales meeting or sales call, as I prefer to call it.

Similarly, it is easy, when selling, to abide by rules that everyone feels to be in place. Yet surprising a customer can add to the force of your message in a competitive situation. After all, if you are involved in a business-to-business tender situation you want to stand out from the crowd. By definition any examples I give you of this have been used before; but they may trigger some thoughts and, after all, not everyone you are selling to will have succumbed to my campaign and bought and read this book.

So you could try one of these unusual openings or activities; they have all worked for the people who told me about them.

Then we turn to the more blanket way of creating interest – the marketing campaign.

Idea 10 – Use surprise to demonstrate technological excellence

I understand that IBM once delivered their response to tender for a public telephone exchange system in a safe. The puzzled customer tried in vain to find the combination and rang up IBM in some annoyance to complain that he could not get to their offer. 'Are we on the short list?' replied IBM. 'Of course not,' said the customer, 'We cannot draw up the short list until we have looked at all the proposals including yours'. 'Ah,' said IBM, 'Our proposals include information on technology that is not released to the public as yet and is years ahead of our competitors and therefore top secret. If you are talking to a lot of manufacturers the information is bound to leak. In any case some competitors may be making a wild proposal based on old technologies that give them a cheap and cheerful solution and may in that way get on to the short list.

'We are happy to share this information when you have got the list down to a few because we know that when you give the proposals serious consideration we will win hands down, and the information leak will not be so important. You can have the combination number of the safe when you confirm that we are on the short list.'

An interesting gamble this, given that the customer may just be irritated by the arrogance of the approach, but a reasonable risk, I think, since the customer is also going to be intrigued to see what the new technology does. Anyway, in the example quoted to me it worked and IBM was on the short list and won the business. The additional benefit the surprise opening gave them was that the amount of work they had to do to win the business was very much reduced since the other companies had to battle to get on to the short list in a campaign that took three months.

Idea 11 – Use surprise to get people to read your mailshot

Junk mail and spam are the two words most used by customers and prospects to describe the unsolicited mail that arrives by post or e-mail – the poor old salesperson calls it a mailshot or a fax shot. We know that most of it *Using surprise* ends up in the waste paper bin and that it is very difficult to get recipients *here gener-* even to read the title before putting it there. Using surprise here generally *ally means* means encouraging the prospect to respond because they are intrigued by *encouraging* something that is on offer. *the prospect*

A company that sells machine tools sent out many mailshots to pro- *to respond* duction engineers. Knowing the nature of the animal receiving the letters, *because they* they made up an inexpensive working model of a machine in kit form. *are intrigued by* When the engineers put the machine together from the bits in the kit, *something that* they discovered that there was either a bit missing or that they had made *is on offer.* a mistake. This made large numbers of them contact the company to find out the truth or complain about the deficiency. The response was much better than other attempts to get the name and number of engineer prospects. Notice how this is also an idea that depends on the ability of the salesperson to understand what makes their customers tick.

Idea 12 – Keep your marketing up to date with real trends

The general competitive pressures in business continue to ratchet up. Productivity increases, technological innovation and the emergence of new players in the business of producing commodities, all combine to increase the pressure on marketing people to find new areas for growth and salespeople to take on higher and higher targets.

Then there is globalisation. The move towards global brands and international account management has been steady over the long term but is getting faster and faster.

So the marketing function has to research much more widely and build communications and feedback systems from remote countries. The need for co-ordination emphasizes also the need for a marketing strategy that is understood and accepted by all parts of the business.

Salespeople in turn need to build international account plans and it is as much their job to sell these internally as it is to sell them to the customer.

The main problem that concerns both functions is that of differentiation. Commodity sales, such as the hardware that makes up computers and workstations, have lower and lower margins as the basic product becomes a commodity.

The gross margin for hardware in the computer industry, for example, has dropped from 55% to somewhere between 15 and 20% over the last 20 years. This change has brought havoc to the sales and marketing function. They are either going to be a commodity broker buying and selling components or complete systems to a market whose sole differentiator is price, or they are going to discover new ways of adding value to the basic product.

Added value one day can be a simple industry standard the following day; so the other big real trend to watch for in the sales and marketing function is the need for huge flexibility, the welcoming of re-training and learning new skills and the ability to accept that doing your job well tomorrow will not be the same as doing it well today.

Note my careful use of the term 'real trends'. It is also quite easy to see a trend where there is a blip or a management fad. This can lead to dips in the creation of interest which, for a major brand, can be very serious.

Idea 13 – Follow the right fads

This is mainly an idea for business-to-business selling. In talking to your customers and prospects when is it useful in creating interest to display a passing knowledge of management ideas, trends or as many of then are – fads?

This is part of a big question of fashion and herd-like movement. Everyone agrees, for example, that the stock market moves on totally emotional grounds like a flock of sheep. Most people agree that there is money to be made out of going against any popular fad in buying and selling shares – being a contrarian. There may well be a parallel in creating interest in your product solutions. Take two strategic fads, the one to diversify in the 1980s, and go back to core business in the 1990s.

If you had been a contrarian in the 1980s you would have gone into the nineties with a fit, slimmed-down business with its eye on its own best focus. This would probably have made you recession-proof in the debacle of the early nineties, with enough debt but not too much and so on. If, however, you had gone against the tide in the nineties, you would have had strong growth in that time but missed out on the revolution that increased the spend on IT and gave huge productivity and customer service benefits.

Unfortunately, the best answer to this question is:

- Keep abreast of business fads.
- Study those you feel might benefit your selling.
- Discuss the ones that make objective business sense and leave the rest to the dedicated followers of fashion.

Take the example of the technology salesperson. You can create interest in your offerings on the grounds of globalisation, knowledge management, being part of the learning organisation, business re-engineering or even 'Who moved my chalk?' And you can sell any of these without changing your products or services one iota – just alter the selling proposition or benefit statements. These fads have all at some point attracted the attention of the business community, which is after all what you are trying to do in this part of the selling process.

Idea 14 – Use technological progress in every part of your marketing effort

This is a huge issue. Facets of it occur in many of the questions raised in this book. I think that you should look for technological progress in every part of the marketing function. The table below shows an example of some of the activities within the marketing function, along with the skills and knowledge needed to carry them out.

Marketing topic	Examples of skills and techniques needed	Examples of knowledge needed
Create a customer-focused analysis of our capabilities and opportunities	SWOT analysis Customer attribute analysis Team planning	Economic trends Technology trends Regulatory trends Competitive environment Customer environment
Defining the company purpose and the marketing strategy	Lateral thinking Long-term planning	What is happening in our chosen markets? What capabilities do we need to be successful?
Market segmentation	Techniques for segmenting markets Documentation methodologies	What type of selling does each segment need? What is the current focus and profitability of each sector?
Goal setting	Producing relevant performance measures Goal setting and documentation Making a business case	What resources are available? What external organisations can help? Calculating return on investment
Action planning	Documenting and maintaining plans Allocating accountability	

The challenge is to assess the impact of technology in every single one of those areas, from using the Internet to gain information on trends to using the intranet to document plans and make them available to the entire organisation.

Idea 15 – Make sure new products fit the brand name

If you want to go into a new market with a new product it is unwise to assume that the brand name that works well for existing products will do just as well for the new ones. An 'upscale', to use the American term, or 'posh', to use the British, car was not on Ford's price list for many years. When they decided to sell one, they realised that the Ford name would not sell well to that market. So, instead of building their own new car, which they could certainly have done, they preferred to buy other marques such as Jaguar and Range Rover.

Creating interest with a brand name is a self-fulfilling disaster if the deeply entrenched message of the brand conflicts with the selling proposition of the product.

Idea 16 – Make your friends your customers

Whenever a person starting a business meets someone, they look for contacts. They want any way they can to get a name to whom they could try and sell something. Drop into any 'Community of Consultants' network of people who are trying to make it on their own and you will see the living proof of that statement. They will pay polite attention to the various products and services in your portfolio, but in the end what they want is contacts. The old story of Amway is an interesting perspective on this, as two people built a business by getting people to sign up to sell Amway products to – guess who – their own friends, relatives and neighbours.

Rich DeVos and Jay Van Andel met in high school and found themselves at one with their views on the American dream. 'The business of America is business,' remarked Calvin Coolidge and DeVos and Van Andel were determined to prove him right. They were sure that it was possible for anyone who put the energy and work in to own his or her own business and grow it to the size they preferred. They resolved to work together towards their dream when they finished military service.

Their first venture was a drive-in restaurant, but it was after a break to sail in South America that their first real success came when they became independent distributors of Nutrilite vitamins. Their version of the American dream evolved into the realisation that direct person-to-person marketing could build a business fast.

Their version of the American dream evolved into the realisation that direct person-to-person marketing could build a business fast.

Real growth, they discovered, would come when they attracted others into the selling side of the business. Using the same person-to-person method they recruited distributors for their new company Amway. The method was described in the Amway Sales and Marketing Plan and told future distributors how to start selling and getting their own distributors. To begin with the main product these channels sold was a multi-purpose cleaner.

By the early 1960s the business outgrew the owners' basements, and they expanded into new premises. In its first year of business Amway sold more than half a million dollars' worth of product. Growth was rapid in all areas, but it is when you look at the ratio of employees to distributors that you see the potential of pushing out to more and more friends and acquaintances to bring them into the distributing fold. By the end of the 1960s they offered 200 products and had 700 employees. The number of distributors in the US and Canada who were, in the jargon of the company, 'building Amway businesses' had reached 100,000.

The 1970s was a decade of further huge growth starting from an annual turnover of $100 million. It was also at this time that the company finally proved to the FTC that Amway offered a genuine business opportunity and was not involved in 'pyramid selling'.

Amway's Ada facility was more than a mile long with all the attributes of a town, including power generation, water treatment, recycling, buses and a fire department.

The product line continued to grow with Nutrilite dietary supplements and the Personal Shoppers catalogues allowing further diversification. By the end of the 1970s there were literally millions of distributors, not only in North America but also in Australia, the UK and Hong Kong.

In 1980 the company turnover broke the billion dollar barrier and more plant was added to keep up with demand. Another new product direction followed, with the introduction of the Amway Water Treatment System, distributed in the same way as before.

Amway defines a customer as a person who buys Amway products but who is not a distributor. He or she is probably introduced to the product by a relative or a friend who is trying to make money out of the Water Treatment product by setting up a business as a distributor. Distributors are always looking for customers but would much prefer to create new distributors.

This is what happens if you would like to become an Amway Water Treatment distributor. You approach, or more likely are approached by, an existing Amway distributor who becomes your 'sponsor'.

The selling is done by the sponsor, talking about the success they are enjoying and, of course, about what benefits the product is bringing to them personally. The sponsor also shows the potential distributor a video that, amongst other things, includes a series of endorsements from the most eminent people that can be found to agree to do it. At one point in the UK, the video included an MP's wife with the politician himself in the background. At some point the prospective distributor will be provided with the Amway Business Kit containing basic Amway products and literature for use in making sales.

The prospect is then invited to produce his or her first prospect list. This is a long list of all the people that they know, from relatives to close friends, colleagues at their current or old workplace and anyone else who might conceivably buy Amway products. The sponsor then goes through the list and probably keeps a copy in case you drop out. The sponsor also helps you to sort your people into good, medium and poor prospects by discussing their income level, lifestyle and so on.

You then place an order for the products you wish to buy and for some stock. You are required to pay for your products immediately but have time to pay for the stock as you, it is to be hoped, sell them. You make money out of your sales to customers and so does your sponsor and his in turn.

You are encouraged to aim at a balance of merchandising Amway products to customers and sponsoring distributors. In the words of the company, 'Amway distributors who sponsor others have higher average sales than those who don't sponsor. Your 'group' is the team of distributors you've sponsored. Many you've sponsored personally, but others were sponsored by those you personally sponsored in the first place. You train and motivate your group and, as a result, you earn extra income when they earn income. As you continue to grow your business and they continue to grow theirs, you both can benefit.' Don't forget, this is person-to-person selling and, despite appearances, not pyramid selling. You are supposed to be building a business.

Amway offers over 450 unique, high quality products whose brand names include Nutrilite™ vitamins and food supplements, Artistry™ skin care and colour cosmetics, eSpring™ system, Magna Bloc™ therapeutic magnets and SA8™ laundry system.

Today, more than 3.6 million independent business owners distribute Amway products in more than 80 countries and territories. Amway is part of the Alticor family of companies, whose global sales totalled $4.5 billion in its most recent fiscal year.

Anything you can do by hard copy literature you can do better by the Internet. Unfortunately, these are mainly scams or as near to scams as makes no difference to the person losing money.

A popular one right now is a ladies-only club where each new lady gives £3000, an amount carefully placed to be inside the tax-free gift regime, and then recruits her friends and relatives with the lure of a lot of money when their turn comes to be a the top of the list. People do and have made money out of such schemes but always the people in on the ground floor. Eventually, of course, the thing has to fizzle out because the chain has to be broken at some point, since people willing to join such a thing become fewer and fewer as the actual recruits increase. Finally they collapse, with the last people in losing all of their £3000. It sounds awfully like pyramid selling again to me, but somehow they get away with it because the donations are regarded as gifts.

It is a great idea, however, since, would you believe, some people despite their experience the first time actually do it again.

There are out there a lot of middle-aged executives who have retired early and have the personality and energy to be good salespeople. Must be a tempting market for any budding Amway lookalike.

Idea 17 – The old ones are sometimes the best ones

Why it can possibly work I do not know, but the old openings by roofers, and builders who lay down private house driveways still seem to do the job. Does anyone believe that someone just passing 'Happened to notice a few tiles loose on your roof', or that because they are working in your area they 'Can give you a very good price'?

And yet such approaches still work. They often work, however, on the elderly or the bewildered; so if you start to use them be aware of whom your bedfellows are. A friend of mine's father was talked into buying tarmac from a team of two road builders who told him that it was spare after their work on a nearby motorway. As it happens the materials changed hands at a fair price, but after it was dropped in a load on the old man's drive the two expressed surprise when the customer seemed to expect them to spread it out over the drive area. This cost much more; if not an arm and a leg, then certainly a leg.

Idea 18 – Use your own money to sell your goods

It is still certainly true that if you want to sell infrastructure products to one of the old Soviet Union countries, you have to have a financial backer behind you. This will be the World Bank, or a world organisation of some sort, or a national bank from the same country as the supplier. It is a variation on an idea that was crucial to opening up the Chinese market. We could not have sold anything to them had it not been for letters of credit.

Idea 19 – Use channels

Inventors market most new products or services themselves in the first place. As quickly as possible, however, it is a good idea to look for partners or new channels of distribution. It will cost a discount or a commission, but is probably the fastest way to get a new idea off the ground.

The Ten Greatest Sales Ideas for Establishing Need

Introduction

Good selling is solution selling. The starting point of solution selling is establishing need – really understanding what the customer needs, and preferably wants. Good establishment of need is predicated on never making assumptions. The starting point is that you do not know what the customer needs until you see things from their point of view. That way you will avoid getting it wrong in a major way and wasting everyone's time including your own.

Put simply, it is a question of questions – asking lots of open questions that reveal the problem or opportunity that uncovers the need for your products or services.

Idea 20 – Avoid a major gaffe

Before we turn to more positive techniques and stories it is worth learning what we can in theory from some dreadful efforts in practice. In the end they keep coming down to seeing everything from the customer's point of view.

Two stories from the car industry remind us that gaffes come from overconfidence as much as from inexperience.

After the Second World War and well into the fifties Britain believed thoroughly in its own industrial propaganda. We thought that British was indeed best. We believed that the UK produced quality products and that, for example, anything from Hong Kong or Japan was an inefficient copy of a good old British product. This led to some bizarre decisions and, of course, to the eventual death, after costing lots and lots of taxpayers' money, of the home-owned car business.

There was a huge craze to export to new countries. One that the car industry selected for the 'British is best' treatment was Brazil. The car maker Austin exported its models to that country and prided itself on meeting customer needs better than its competitors by actually translating the owner's manual into Spanish. Elementary market research might have given them the news that the principal language in Brazil is Portuguese.

Equally arrogant was the export of the Morris Minor, a car sold in exceptional numbers worldwide, also to South America. They went to the trouble of finding out that South American car owners wanted lots of chrome on their cars, inside and out, and produced a special export model that included just that. Okay, sounds like they are meeting needs. But they could not believe that the market would find any inconvenience in the fact that the door locks on the left-hand drive models they sold abroad remained on the right-hand side of the vehicle. In the case of the models sold to South America this meant, of course, that in order to get into their car the proud owner had to go round to the passenger's side of the car, unlock the door, stretch across to open the driver's door from the inside and go back round to the driver's side to get in. Lots of cars gleaming with chrome were left on the forecourts of Argentina, Chile and other points south.

Idea 21 – Ask your customers about their business case

I have had some good debates with the finance departments of many clients whose salespeople I have been teaching this technique. In essence, all the salesperson does is make enquiries into how the client calculates and proves its business case before it makes a buying decision. Many clients will try to knock you back when you ask saying that it is commercially confidential; but most can be persuaded to share the process with you, since your experience with other clients who have invested in your product or service may add to the new client's understanding of the benefits side of the cost–benefit analysis.

Why do many salespeople avoid this issue, running a mile when their input is sought about the likely cost–benefit analysis the customer should be doing? Mainly, I think, because of fear of not being able to make a contribution. Why do they have that fear? Because we are talking about the future here and the unknown impact that a new process or technique is going to have on the bottom line of the business.

If you think of it in selling terms it may get easier. How does a sales manager, Sally, decide whether or not to give one of her account managers more sales resources? The account manager is keen to get the extra resource, since he knows that there is more business in his account if he could cover the ground more effectively. The sales manager is happy to find the money for the new person, but has to be convinced that she is putting her scarce resources into the most productive area. So the answer to the first question, 'Will you sell more if we put another salesperson on your patch?' is easy: 'Sure we will.' The second question is much more difficult: 'How much more?' Now consider what is going through the account manager's mind. He knows that if he claims a very high figure, say $5 million, Sally may be sceptical but will probably be sufficiently impressed to let him have the resource. But at what cost? She will, of course, change the estimate into a management objective, and the account manager's target will go up by $5 million or an amount which recognizes that it will take a while to get the new person up to speed.

If, on the other hand, the account manager goes low, saying: 'Well, for the first year I think we must allow a settling in period and maybe expect $100,000', there are probably other account managers who will offer Sally a better deal than this and she will prefer to give them the resource. So he has to go somewhere between these two. He wants to be successful and to be seen to be successful. This means that he would rather take a target of $900,000 and make $950,000, than take a target of $1 million and get $950,000 – the first is success, the second is failure. And so his thoughts go on. He will try to agree a number that he really believes he can achieve, but will be attractive enough to get his manager's agreement to the hiring of the

Why do many salespeople avoid this issue, running a mile when their input is sought about the likely cost–benefit analysis the customer should be doing?

person. Funnily enough, although this seems a rather political and illogical way of making a decision, if the people involved are any good at their jobs, their estimates will probably be quite reasonable.

Exactly the same debate goes on if the managers involved are in the production area or research and development or whatever. A salesperson should not feel inhibited about getting involved in a discussion of this nature.

Idea 22 – Think like a fish

This is how a seasoned business-to-business salesperson put it: 'I am a fisherman and to be successful it pays to "think like a fish".' This same technique has always stood me in good stead in the sales situation: think like your customer – put yourself in his position and see how your offering/solution stacks up. How does it get him nearer to achieving his goals?

Idea 23 – Don't push if he doesn't want it

Here's a tip from a project manager who found himself in situations where he had to try to convince people that his solution was a good one and that they should come on board. 'If it looks like you want the thing more than they need it you will put them off. At some point walk away and see if they follow, where pushing towards them might make them back away.'

Idea 24 – Make the product irrelevant to the sale

At first glance this appears almost the opposite of properly establishing need. What happens in this situation is that the salesperson appeals to an emotion or instinct that overwhelms the customer into buying, despite their having no need or want for the product. *Big Issue* salespeople use it frequently when they hold up one copy of their magazine in the shopping mall and shout to the passers-by, 'Big Issue, help the homeless, come on people just the one left and I can finish for the day.' Someone buys it, not because they need the magazine but because they need or want to help the homeless and let the guy get back to wherever he is going. It works every time on my daughter, even though she knows that once she is round the corner with her purchase a 'second' last copy will remarkably appear.

Idea 25 – Don't miss the main need

An experienced sales trainer told me that no matter how important they know it is, all salespeople forget that a sale is made because of a customer need not because of a product's brilliance. He illustrates it as follows, pointing out that although this is a very simple mistake that no one would make, when we sell our own products we fall into the same trap as Mr John Cleese.

'John Cleese does a very good illustration of what establishing need is about. It is very funny since, in his annoying way, he is standing on his market stall, and the product he is selling is water. He is impatient with prospective buyers, although he is fantastically enthusiastic. An old couple in their seventies arrive at the stall, hand in hand, and ask John what exactly water is! Cleese goes into a most extraordinary sales pitch. "Well", he says, "you can use water all over the place. You can water your garden with it, and thus make the flowers healthy, and keep the grass green. You can bathe in it with hot water, which makes you clean and tidy. You can mix it with soap, and clean your clothes. You can apply it to your car, and keep it clean." He continues to talk enthusiastically about his product. The old man tries to ask him questions, but John is in full flow, and cannot be stopped from shouting his wares. The old man then starts to turn away. John Cleese is flummoxed in his customary way, angry that another potential but stupid customer cannot see the benefits of the product. The old lady says to her husband, "You know I thought that product was really good, why didn't you buy it?" "Well," he says, "What I really want is a drink."

'The moral of the story, from a selling point of view, is that you have two ears and one mouth, and salespeople should use them in proportion. The other lesson to be learned, is although you may be enthusiastic about the product, if the customer doesn't want it, you are wasting your time. The easiest way to sell someone a spade is to persuade them that they need to dig a hole.'

The easiest way to sell someone a spade is to persuade them that they need to dig a hole.

Idea 26 – Use endorsements

Most consultants, tradesmen and many salespeople get almost all of their new business customers from endorsements from people who have used them before. The professionally produced list of previous and satisfied customers is a must for any prospecting salesperson. Remember, though, that it is not just satisfaction with the product and your ability to deliver it for which you need a reference. People want to know that someone did get a benefit out of the product or service they bought. In business-to-business selling this normally means return on investment. Make sure that your reference brochures include a quotation from a customer explaining how things changed after they became a customer and what the bottom-line benefit was.

An interesting variation on this is the endorsement by a seemingly independent body. You find it, for example, in medical selling, where an endorsement by the British Dental Association that fluoride is good for your children may help toothpaste manufacturers to sell their unique 'it's all in the stripe'.

Idea 27 – Make sure you want as well as need the business

Everybody with an iota of selling instinct in their bodies wants an opportunity to sell, particularly if it is a massive opportunity. I was talking recently to a managing director of a company that takes on big government systems integration projects. He mentioned with a tremor in his voice that the Government had come out to tender for a project which, over ten years, was worth something like £5 billion. I said that I understood his concern; bidding for such a big deal must be very frightening. 'Oh,' he said, 'I am not worried about going through the tendering process, I'm worried about winning the business.' I know he was half joking; but it does make the point that we should only go for it if, as a result of winning, we are not getting more problems than the contract is worth. Anyway, the man's a salesman, so they're going for it.

ABC – Always be closing

Need any consultancy help for planning the £5bn sales campaign, Bill?

Idea 28 – Where there is a need there is an opportunity

We have said that everybody lives by selling something. Equally, anything that has a value can be sold. When an expatriate in a country that does not permit the public sale of alcoholic drinks leaves to go home, they sell any equipment that can be used to produce alcohol – if it is legal of course – to whoever is coming in next. It's a bit like selling the job of the doorman at the Savoy Hotel – that is worth a lot of money.

Idea 29 – As a last resort take action to create the need

I cannot leave a section on establishing need without reporting one of the most famous sales interviews that has passed into selling folklore.

A sales manager was choosing between two salespeople who were on the short list applying for one job. Unable to decide between the two, he withdrew a pen from his pocket, gave it to the first salesman and asked him to sell it to him.

'This is an excellent writing implement,' said the first salesman, 'Ideal for when you need something to write with without notice. Look at the transparent barrel holding the ink. It is transparent so that you can see at a glance when it is running out and replace it before you hit the embarrassing situation of being unable to write when you need to. It also has this cap to it with a hook that latches over your pocket top making it portable and unobtrusive at the same time. The cap has a second function too – you take it off to write and place it on the end of the barrel. This gives you a slightly heavier and more balanced writing implement. Notice also the little stopper at the end. This is important to prevent leakage of the ink. If, for example, it were to leak while you were carrying the pen in your pocket, you may get an expensive cleaning bill if the ink goes on to the material of your suit. This stopper prevents that. Finally, there is the ballpoint mechanism itself, ensuring a consistent supply of ink to the paper, giving you clear, attractive writing for others to read.'

The sales manager was impressed. The man had identified many features of a simple product and turned each one into a benefit. One of the benefits, cleaning bill avoidance, even had a cost justification element. Thinking that he would have a big problem following that, the manager turned to the second salesman and gave him the same pen and the same challenge. The salesman took the pen, grasped it between both hands, snapped it in half and said, 'You need a new one.'

The Seven Greatest Sales Ideas for Selling Through an Agreed Basis of Decision

Introduction

These ideas are all about presenting your sales pitch in the context of the client's real issues, as opposed to banging the gong of product features.

After completing her university degree, a young relative of mine was applying, somewhat reluctantly, for a job in industry or commerce. She was reluctant because her burning desire was to be an orchestral musician. Persuaded by parents and teachers, however, she applied for a number of 'real' jobs, in the 'real' world outside music. She asked me, in my role as an experienced businessman, to look through her application forms.

One of her applications was to a newspaper and magazine publisher for a job as a trainee journalist. To my horror, and I'm afraid amusement, she had replied to the question 'What newspapers and magazines do you regularly read' with one word – 'None'.

In terms of selling herself to the organisation, my niece was ignoring the corporation's probable 'basis of decision'. It is certain that a newspaper and magazine publisher is going to make it a key criterion for a journalist that 'they must be interested enough to read a cross-section of newspapers and magazines regularly'.

The basis of decision is about what people really want personally. When she was applying for the job in journalism, my niece was in fact ignoring her own basis of decision. The key criterion for her working life was not 'the job must involve reading and writing newspapers and magazines' but rather, 'the job must involve playing the viola'. And bit by bit, I'm glad to say she's getting there.

Because it's taken outside the context of our own selling space, such a failure to think through the client's basis of decision seems laughable to most salespeople. Yet in their everyday selling lives and in their proposals, brochures and letters, many salespeople still ignore the basis of decision. They still prefer to hit the client with a series of product features, advantages and benefits.

And yet the basis of decision is a much subtler and more user-friendly way of going about the selling job. It is usable in four distinct parts of the sales cycle – establishing need, making a proposal, handling price objections and discussing wins and losses. First of all; what is it?

Idea 30 – Break the basis of decision into three points

Establishing the basis of decision (BoD) is said by many to be the key technique that distinguishes the solution seller from the product seller. It involves understanding from the client's point of view all the issues surrounding the sale. It is often useful to divide the criteria that make up the BoD into three parts, the financial, technical and practical basis of decision.

In today's climate it is easy to imagine that the financial basis of decision is simply: 'We will buy the cheapest.' This can be very unsatisfactory from the seller's point of view as it erodes margins and obviously can only allow one winner – the cheapest. It can also be unsatisfactory from the buyer's point of view as it ignores other potential differences in the competitive proposals on offer – the features of the product and the service surrounding delivery and implementation – the technical and practical issues. In the final idea in this section we will look at a technique that aims systematically to establish that what the buyer is getting is the best value for money.

Idea 31 – Use the basis of decision to establish need

In addition to gaining information on the problems for which the potential client wants to buy an answer, the solution-selling salesperson makes sure they agree the BoD at the time they establish need.

The conversation about the financial basis of decision must aim at 'best value for money'. The salesperson may even suggest that from experience their company may not make the lowest offer, but that they still tend to win the business by offering superior features and service. If sellers cannot move the client from preferring the cheapest at this stage, and they know that they will not be the cheapest, they can offer to withdraw. Frequently such an offer will reawaken the client's interest in matters apart from cost. All part of professional establishment of the client's real needs.

You are seeing the thing from the customer's point of view – always the most powerful way to make a point.

Suppose you are selling insurance to retailers. If, for example, the Professional Negligence Section of your Opticians Practices policy is underwritten at Lloyd's, and you believe that the competition's may not be, it may be worth trying to get into the BoD that the client is prepared to pay slightly more for the benefit of Lloyd's; after all, it's the only underwriter everyone has heard of. It is much easier to get logical agreement to this at an early stage, rather than when the competitive offerings are on the prospect's desk. Notice how, by getting their agreement to the offer being underwritten by Lloyd's into the BoD, you are not slagging off the competition or yelling about your product. You are, on the contrary, seeing the thing from the customer's point of view – always the most powerful way to make a point. And you are doing it at the best time in the selling process.

Moving to the technical basis of decision, much of the discussion will be around the insurance cover required. Here, too, the salesperson should be leaning towards seeing the issues as though they were in the customer's shoes rather than banging on about the product specification. Use phrases like, 'So you need cover against business interruption, and your computer equipment should be detailed separately. You do not require insurance for loss of money in transit.' This is subtly more user-friendly than 'Our policy covers business interruption, computer equipment as a separate detail and loss of money in transit.' What you are trying to do, as usual, is to see it from the client's point of view rather than the product brochure, thus keeping everything relevant.

And finally we come to using the practical basis of decision in establishing need. The broader this is, the better the chance of having issues apart from cost included in the decision.

Here are a few of examples of the practical basis of decision suggested by a seller of insurance policies to Opticians Practices:

- The package should include all principal business needs in one policy.
- The administrators of the scheme must have a lot of experience in your type of business.
- The insurance cover must be tailored to your business without losing its cost-competitiveness.
- The underwriters must be first rank UK-based companies.

It is likely that salespeople will include these statements in their selling document, but getting the phraseology put in the client's terms can give competitive edge.

In a complex sale made over a period of time, it is good selling practice to send out a Basis of Decision letter after the fact finding and establishing need exercise has been carried out. This will state the BoD and who from the client has agreed it. Any competitive edge which the seller has will be much more compelling stated as the prospect's BoD rather than as a puff in the 'Why buy it from us' section of the proposal.

Idea 32 – Use the basis of decision in making written proposals

Following the template in the figure, the solution seller writes a proposal or a letter as the selling part of the offer. Notice where the basis of decision comes in the argument – before the benefit statements – and you can see the subtle but powerful difference in presentation.

Template for a written proposal

Scope of the proposal

Customer problem or opportunity

Solution

Benefits

Implementation plan

Recommended action

Example of a basis of decision as part of a selling document

An insurance seller is making a proposal to a large antiques and fine art dealer. Rather than simply reproducing claims on the brochure that the salesperson's company has a lot of experience with such businesses, the seller uses the BoD technique to gain competitive edge. Here are some examples:

'During our discussion with Mr A and Ms B we have agreed the following key issues in assessing possible providers of insurance cover:

- 'You need a policy administrator with experience in dealing with companies and people in the antiques and fine art business.
- 'As well as the normal cover for a retail organisation, you need to protect yourself from defective title, where loss results from goods purchased which subsequently turn out to be stolen.
- 'You wish to take advantage of any Association discounts.'

It is then apparent that the client is pulling at the desired features of the seller's offering rather than the seller pushing them. When they get to the benefits section, the seller modestly accepts that they can meet the detailed and strict requirements of the client.

Idea 33 – Use the basis of decision to handle price objections

'Sorry, mate, I've found a cheaper quote.' What do you do when you hear these words? Most industries have always been price-sensitive and it has never been more so than now. Intermediaries and even consumers, who can use the Internet, can trawl for the cheapest price. There is a huge impact on the bottom line of giving away, for example, any of the commission percentage an insurance broker earns from a sale, so salespeople need a cleverer method of selling the value of the product and of their service. Basis of decision selling provides just that technique.

Consider the possible answers to the above question. 'We'll match it' gives the profit problem. A re-iteration of the features and benefits of the salespersons proposal sounds heavy, is probably boring, and clients are unlikely to be swayed at this stage. In any case, at this stage they think that the alternative offer is similar. Much better is to drive back to the basis of decision. Try the return question 'If we were the same price as the quote you are preferring just now, would you buy from us?'

What is the client to say? Suppose they say, 'Well, no actually' – the worst outcome – at least you can now ask why, and deal with the other objections, real or imagined. Suppose they say, 'Well, yes I think we would.' At that point the same question 'Why?' will elicit what the client believes are your advantages as opposed to your general statements. In this case clients are almost persuading themselves that the bit extra is worth it. Incidentally, the other selling technique tested by this method of handling price objections is the ability to remain silent. Frequently the 'Would you buy from us if we were the same price as the cheapest?' question leads to a lot of thought from the prospect. Keep your mouth shut and wait for the response.

Idea 34 – Use the basis of decision to discuss wins and losses

The glory of winning, and the pain of losing, often make us forget to learn the lessons of past campaigns. The salesperson that does this improves rapidly. Simply put, if your product was up to the job, and you lost, you misunderstood the basis of decision. Go back in, or have one more telephone call. Don't complain if you lost or crow if you won, but do ask how the decision was made. Re-establish the real BoD.

Idea 35 – Identify real 'value for money'

Idea 36 looks at the process involved in selling value for money, particularly business-to-business selling or selling within an organisation, but it is worth looking at this as a basic skill in dealing with customers. Here is one of my experiences as an independent consultant that makes the point well.

For many years I have offered consultancy services from a company that consists only of me. I am a one-man band. I did a planning job once for a big electricity company. The job was phase one of three phases and the customer and I completed it successfully. Indeed, the main customer sponsor was delighted. When it came to phase two, the amount of money at stake meant that according to their purchasing rules they had to go out to tender. My sponsor was pushed towards inviting in McKinseys who were doing a lot of work at the time at holding board level, as well as getting me to bid for the work. I was only working at the operating company board level.

So look at what you provide in terms of your customer's perception of value and you will understand how to approach them and how, if this is part of your function, to price it.

Now, since they had used my processes for phase one, it made almost no sense at all to change consultants for the second part of the project. I knew this, of course, and decided to go in at the highest price I dared. I really loaded my quote and waited for the reaction. It came from a telephone call from the sponsor. He sounded concerned and embarrassed and I feared the worst. 'Ken,' he said, 'I've got a problem with your price.' 'Oh my God,' thought I, 'I've overcooked it,' and I started stammering about how I could probably take another look at it. The customer agreed with this and suggested that I took another person on to the project and 'Make it more of a team approach.' 'But,' I said, 'That will make it more expensive.' 'I know, Ken. The problem is you are more than £200,000 lower than the McKinsey quote. I can't take your number in as it is, the purchasing people will laugh you out of court.'

So I took another guy on and shoved the price up to what was for me a stratospheric height. I got the business and boy did we holiday well that year.

What has happened here? My original quote reflected the amount of time I had to put into the project and the price gave me a good return on that time. McKinsey went in at a price that reflected their knowledge, access to expertise and their reputation. One could speculate at this time that neither bid really reflected the value that the project would bring to the customer. It is that value that eventually won the day.

So look at what you provide in terms of your customer's perception of value and you will understand how to approach them and how, if this is part of your function, to price it. The carrot for doing this, as we have seen, is that your value as perceived by them may be much more than you realise. The stick is that if you put a higher value on your performance than they do you are living in a fool's paradise and are risking losing that particular customer.

Idea 36 – Prove that the customer is getting 'value for money'

Here is a technique based on a simple spreadsheet for listing a customer's criteria for decision and weighting the response of a number of competitors. It is almost the epitome of basis of decision selling, since it could very well be the technique a buyer would use for making a buying decision. Except, of course, that you, the seller, draw it up. It is even better if the seller assists the customer to draw up the list and the results have a chance of removing the objectivity that the customer thinks they are bringing to the exercise.

Criteria	Weighting	Us	W. avg	Competitor 1	W. avg	Competitor 2	W. avg
1	25	4	1.00	3	0.75	5	1.25
2	40	3	0.75	4	1.00	3	0.75
3	10	2	0.50	1	0.25	1	0.25
4	10	1	0.25	1	0.25	2	0.50
5	15	3	0.75	2	0.50	4	1.00
			69%		64%		73%

Put the five principal decision criteria in the first column. Now, remembering to do this from the customer's point of view, estimate the importance of each criterion against each other and mark each with a percentage. The most important criteria in the case in Figure Idea 36 is the second one, which is given a weighting of 40%. Notice how the total weightings come to 100.

Now give yourself a mark between 0 and 5 as an estimate of how well you fare against each of these criteria. Do the same for the competition. The next column takes the mark you have given each supplier against each criterion and produces the weighted average. Finally, the total at the bottom of the weighted average gives a percentage for each supplier. In the example, we are not as well placed to win the business as competitor 2, and we would be well advised either to get the customer to agree a different weighting or to change our proposal. Incidentally, you can also use this system to forecast the chance factor of winning a bid. In this case competitor 2 has a 73% chance of winning the business, but is closely pursued by two close competitors.

The Eight Greatest Sales Ideas for Presenting Your Case

Introduction

Despite all the listening a salesperson has done during the early part of their sales campaigns, there does come a time when they have to present their solution to the customer. This section looks at the all-important communications between customers and their suppliers.

Idea 37 – Make sure the whole team is talking to customers

The only way to keep your organisation in touch with reality is to allow very few of them to be completely unexposed to customers. You can do this individually by insisting your product developer, for example, attends customer progress meetings, or en masse by inviting the customer to come and speak at the annual get-together. Engineers, for example, sometimes completely transform the way they think about their work when they come to have a real insight into what the customers are trying to do, and how they look at their offerings.

An unlikely contender for customer contact is the finance department. But suppose for a moment that you run the financial control department for an organisation based in several locations, none of which is in your building. You would not consider trying to do that without going to see them on their site to get a feel for what they are contending with. Indeed, if you do not get some of your accounts people out there as well, you are failing to tap into an important source of insights. If the accounts people get out there from time to time, they will probably see activity going on at the site that could be assisted by a simple change in how they carry out their tasks or a modification to their processes that you have missed because of your lack of intimate knowledge of the details.

It is even more important for the accounts department to get direct knowledge of your customers. Get them face to face with customers and be prepared for them to realise the changes they have to make, and for your customers to realise how professional is the whole team serving them.

Idea 38 – Present yourself well

At some point in any sales campaign, be it internal or external, you will probably have to get up on your feet and address the buyers. If you have a natural talent for making presentations and you can enjoy them once the nervousness has worn off, you put yourself ahead of the competition. In some customer cultures, indeed, you are pretty much up against it if your presentations skills are poor or if you look scared witless at the end of the presentation as well as at the beginning. At an early stage in your sales career volunteer to be the person who presents the results of a workshop, or makes a presentation on some new topic to the departmental meeting.

I had no idea of how useful presentations were until this incident happened to me. In the dark ages of the 1970s the business world was burdened with a new tax – Value Added Tax. I was a graduate trainee at the time and my boss, who sometimes found it difficult to think of constructive things for a rookie to do, asked if I could have a look at this VAT business and make a presentation of what it was about to the next Area Meeting. I got hold of government papers and found the concept of the tax hard to understand. I persevered, spoke to a load of people, including government people, who were helpful. At last I was able to understand how the tax worked in my terms. These were, of course, the terms that my colleagues in the area would also use. A bit of luck had me hear a joke on the radio about VAT inspectors being called 'Vatman and Robin', so I nicked that and used it as a running gag through the presentation. It went well and I knew that it had done me no harm at all. My boss mentioned that it had gone well to his boss who told him that he had attended a presentation by some accountants on the tax and that no one in the audience had understood a word of it. I was asked to give the same presentation to the management team at my boss's boss's team meeting – very useful, high profile stuff, and a lesson in influencing people.

If you are not a natural at this game, go on training until you can at least survive, although I do know one senior manager who made it to the top and remained a complete liability on his feet. When asked how he did it he replied, 'Ducking and weaving, old boy, I avoided presentations like the plague.'

Think about your preparation in three areas – the structure of the content or argument, the mechanics of the room and the visual aids, and your personal delivery.

Funnily enough, the usual suspects are the best tips for making effective presentations. Set tight objectives and talk exclusively in the terms of the audience. Try not to talk to mixed audiences. It can be difficult to make the same presentation to the marketing people and research and development at the same time, even though the topic may be of mutual interest.

It is a very good idea to announce the objectives at the start of the presentation. The audience then knows where you are going to take them. Some people avoid this since you do run the risk that someone in the audience will say that it will not be possible for you to achieve your objectives. Logically it is better to know this at the start of the presentation than at the end. Who knows, if you know what the audience's objections are you may be able to use the presentation itself to overcome them. 'Presentations are about them, the audience, rather than you, the speaker,' was how one senior manager put it to me. 'It actually makes you look better when you are talking about them.'

Think about your preparation in three areas – the structure of the content or argument, the mechanics of the room and the visual aids, and your personal delivery.

Structure

Before you start, make sure that it is the right time to make the presentation in the first place. Quite often you could achieve your objectives in some other way that costs less and possibly has less risk. Mind you, if the point of the presentation is to raise your profile in an organisation then ignore this advice. Make sure also that you have done everything possible before the presentation that can help to achieve the objectives. Getting the most senior person on your side before you begin is a good idea. Finally, make sure you know your audience well enough. What will motivate them to think your product or service a good one? What is in it for them? Aim at making effective presentations as well as elegant ones and use your performance on the day to give it a theatrical edge.

Now prepare the background to the presentation. Who asked you to do this? Who have you talked to, and who has helped you? Cover also whose agreement you already have to what you are proposing. The audience should now be aware of how well qualified you are to talk to them on this topic.

Now state the problem or opportunity that you are addressing. You are there to agree that you and your audience have a problem and you have the solution, or that they have an opportunity and you know how to exploit it. If it is difficult to express your purpose as a problem or opportunity then you have not set your objective specifically enough. Always ride your luck, in presentations. If a point has gone down well, consider if you need to work on that one and drop some other points that you have prepared.

Now comes the clever bit of preparation that will set your work ahead of the competition. Get the audience to understand, and if possible agree the 'basis of decision' that they should use in looking at your solution. This is a much more subtle way of selling an idea than banging on about the features of your solution. The basis of decision you suggest will, of course, describe your solution. You are then able at a later time to say simply 'And my suggested action plan meets the basis of decision we spoke about (or agreed) at the beginning of this session.' The more interactive you keep this part, and the more it appears that they have built their own basis of decision, the more likely you are to get their agreement.

Now reveal your solution. Do it in their terms, illustrate it with examples and make sure that at the end of this section the audience will be able to describe exactly how things will be if they adopt your idea. Be open to new ideas. Even if you have spent a lot of time preparing a presentation, you should still listen to your audience and be ready to accept an alternative idea if it is better than yours.

Now hit them with the benefits. These are the business and personal benefits they will get from your proposal. Now they should know what is in it for them

When you are presenting to a customer or prospect, don't mistime the delivery of the section on why they should do business with your particular company. No one is in the least bit interested in your company unless they have provisionally decided that they want to adopt your solution. I am therefore convinced that you should never do the 'Why My Company' fanfare until someone in the audience has asked, 'Why should we go with you on this one?' or words to that effect. Similarly, it is good technique to say the enquirer 'What would you like to know about our organisation?' even if you have a well-prepared pitch. This helps you to tailor your pitch to what the audience thinks is important rather than what you think is important. Sorry to bang on, but I have seen more presentations ruined by overselling the presenter's company at the wrong time than by any other misdemeanour.

The time has come to close for agreement. Make sure you can spell out the next one or two steps that need to be carried out to make progress. If they agree to your future plan they have agreed with your suggestion.

Mechanics

More can go wrong with the mechanics of a presentation than you would believe. I have seen people arrive with visual aids that the room did not have the facilities to show. I have seen piles of overhead projector slides dropped and mixed up, flipchart stands falling over, overhead projector slides slowly curling up until they display nothing and so on. The main messages here are – keep it simple and know the room and rehearse in it beforehand if possible.

Next get the timing right. People do not like presentations going on beyond the time allowed, particularly if you are one item on an agenda. Plan your timing to get to the future plan well before the end of the time allocated. Three-quarters of the way through is perfect, since you then have time to deal with questions and objections. No audience likes to be told to keep their questions to the end. Why should they? If they need an answer to follow your drift they need to ask the question.

If there is more than one speaker at the same meeting there are some further hazards, which is why I much prefer to work on my own. Make sure every speaker has compared notes, and that they are all there for the whole presentation. An audience loves nothing more than one speaker contradicting something a previous speaker said.

Be prepared for the questions you will be asked and objections that will be raised. It is excellent technique to role-play the audience's questions with a colleague at rehearsal time. You will find that you have practised 80% of the questions if you do, and will produce much smoother and more convincing answers as a result. If someone asks a silly question, the rest of the audience will be aware of this and laugh, outwardly or inwardly, at his or her foolishness.

Don't add to their discomfort by scoring a witty point off their stupidity, since, funnily enough, this actually brings the audience back on to the questioner's side and makes them regard you as the sort of person who kicks a person when they are down.

Finally, rehearsal is not optional. If you rush in to give the usual pitch to a new audience without thinking it through and rehearsing, it will look exactly as though that is what you have done.

Presentations have great potential to give good return to the professional sales-person, but as usual they carry the consequent risk. Most of this risk is in the me-chanics of the event.

Anthony Jay, creator of 'Yes, Minister' says, 'If I have to pick just two pieces of advice for business presentations, I would say: "Rehearsal with the role-playing of the question and answer session, and the use of visual aids that are pictures rather than words or figures."'

Delivery

Strange as it may seem, if you set good objectives and get the structure and mechanics right your delivery will not be the make or break of the presentation. This is why many people who do not regard themselves as natural performers can give effective presentations time after time. If you are using the right words in the right order and your visual aids work, most of the battle is done. But there are some rules of thumb that can be useful

The first of these is to check that the talk is interesting. Like, really interesting to the audience not just to you. This rule tends to make presentations shorter rather than longer. The old comic's maxim 'Always leave them wanting more' holds good in selling life. Do not go on if you have achieved your objective. Just because you have prepared another five slides you do not have to use them. I have seen people unsell an idea by going on after they had received agreement to their proposition.

Use spoken rather than written English and try to vary your voice. If you have a tendency to be monotonous, use more than one type of visual aid to gain variety. Move around; sit down from time to time; do anything to keep the audience's attention.

Making the audience laugh is a good thing; telling jokes in the manner of 'I wonder if you have heard the one about …' is bad. Always weave yourself into the story. You met the person who said … or you were in the train with a man who … Even if it is an outrageous gag that you could not possibly have witnessed, they will enjoy the story much more than if you raise a huge signpost saying 'Joke coming'.

Finally, check your delivery for the abstract and avoid it. Talk in simple concrete terms and don't pad it out in any way. Avoid the missed sales of poor presenters by following these simple rules of persuasive communication.

Idea 39 – Look at payment from the customer's point of view

Photocopiers, for example, have made much more money from their users by charging for each copy, paying by the click it is called, than by going through the capital invest-ment route to get the users to buy the actual machines.

Businesses pay for things in two basic ways – out of the capital investment budget or out of their revenue or expenses budget. When you are making your case for expenditure bear this in mind. Photocopiers, for example, have made much more money from their users by charging for each copy, paying by the click it is called, than by going through the capital investment route to get the users to buy the actual machines. The same goes pretty much for anything that is rented rather than bought. So if your organisation has the cashflow to support it, look for ways of earning out of the revenue budget rather than capital expenditure.

It can work the other way round, of course. For example, many pension-ers are increasing their spending ability by raising money secured on their property and paying interest-only payments on the loan. Fundamentally this is not good business, but if the need arises it can solve a problem – or rather, move the problem on by a generation!

The point is to organize your invoices to suit the customer. I used to play on this note with local government customers whose financial year ended in April. My financial year ended in September and that was when I had to have my order book, revenues for the year and cashflow sorted out. From time to time they paid invoices at a time to sort out my cashflow in September, and I held back invoices, or brought them forward, at the end of March.

Idea 40 – Target the decision-maker

This is a much easier idea to write down and explain than it is to carry out. Let us start from a point that is true in most sales that are made to consumers or in business-to-business – any decision that involves a number of people will have one person whose opinion will be most important or paramount to getting a positive decision. It is normally the most senior person but is quite often delegated down the line. The job of the salesperson is to identify that person, make sure they have access to them and agree some key points of the sales campaign with them.

It is particularly important to gain their agreement at certain times in the sales process – establishing agreement and agreeing the basis of decision being the main ones. Apart, that is, from when you ask them for the order.

ABC – Always be closing

A lot of people ask the decision-maker if they are in a position to place the order whenever they meet them. This is good technique since it will sometimes short cut the hoops that technical and practical recommenders are putting the salesperson through.

The reason for the difficulty is that more than one person may believe themselves to be the decision-maker, the actual decision-maker may not agree to meet the salesperson and so on. I have got to the end of long systems integration sales campaigns and not been entirely sure, even after getting the order, who had the most sway over the buying team. Indeed, I have actually been involved in buying capital goods on behalf of a board of directors of which I was a member and even in that instance not been certain of who the real decision-maker was. Sorry about that, but nobody said that life was easy.

We have said that it is best to avoid making presentations to a mixed group of technical assessors, user representatives and the decision-maker. If this is unavoidable, then clearly you should pay most attention to the decision-maker. Here is a cautionary tale in this regard from a senior guy in publishing.

A rising young exec was, for the first time, heading up a presentation team for a large slice of a major corporation's sales promotion budget. Someone at college had told him that in every prospective client audience was a person with the greatest influence over colleagues – not necessarily the CEO, either. Identify, and concentrate on selling to that key person.

Introductions were made, and our hero was confused. Every member of his audience was top-drawer management, dark suited or skirted; all had clipboards or notepads on which he knew that his team's performance would be marked under various headings and compared with the competition. As he started his preamble – his company's background and track record – his eyes were darting around like those of a newcomer to London traffic.

Then the conference room door opened again and in came the man! Tall, tanned, Armani-suited and unencumbered by notebooks or gizmos, he sat quietly apart from the others. Eye contact was made with our hero, and what just qualified as smiles were exchanged. Right! thought our hero.

As he introduced the proposals, PowerPoint slide after slide were accompanied by a charm offensive directed at tall-and-tanned, who responded with increasing eye-twinkles and gratifying nods of the head. After other team members had put on some detail and the budget breakdown, our hero summed up, and his key man almost applauded.

'Well,' said the prospect's marketing director – and as she rose, so did her colleagues – 'we'll be in touch.' And out they went. Forward came tall-and-tanned, hand outstretched to our hero.

'Thank you my boy, that was most interesting,' said he. 'Here's my card – I'm one of your company's major shareholders. Your chairman suggested that I came along to see how you do things. Sorry I was a bit late.'

Idea 41 – If someone says they are a poor presenter, believe them

Generally speaking, most people in business who get to a reasonably high level are good presenters, or at least they can get away with it. There is the occasional exception. I was working with a second line sales manager for whom I had a lot of respect. He was lucid, logical and witty in meetings with or without clients, and socially he was an expert mixer at corporate events.

I had a very important presentation to give to a new client in a competitive situation and I wanted this man's weight behind me. I asked him to say a few words at the beginning of the presentation, just to describe the size and weight of the organisation that was behind my team and me if we got the business. He said that he would prefer not to because he was very poor at making presentations. I didn't really believe him and persuaded him to have a go.

On the day he was extraordinary. He stuttered, lost the place, said the same thing more than once and looked a complete idiot. He had the opposite effect than the one I was looking for. Ever since then if anyone, no matter how senior, tells me that they are uncomfortable making presentations I take their word for it and 'duck and weave' to keep them away from the podium.

Idea 42 – Present the numbers in a way that suits the customer

In the strange world of large organisations the motivation of individuals working in them should never be assumed. A colleague of mine was selling a software package to one of the largest software suppliers in the world. It was a complex deal because the number of users was hard to estimate. Having gone through a process of trying to resolve this, the account manager decided to go back to the old way, which was to charge a set fee per annum, no matter how many users there were in the large organisation.

He set a price. There is no such thing as a price list when you are selling a deal ten times bigger than any other deal your company has done, and he offered a discount of 40% to the Financial Director. This was rejected immediately and the account manager was given a severe message that the FD had gone back in the records and fond that when they paid in this way before, the discount had been 75%.

The salesman put in a new proposal and the FD signed it off. In fact the company was paying £50,000 more with the 75% on a higher price than they were in the original 40% offer. But that was not the point; the FD had protected his company from being ripped off. Who was it who said, 'It's a funny old world'?

Idea 43 – Use the cup of coffee close to present to a committee

Many decisions in business are taken by a group of people, a committee or a board for example, and many a sale has been lost because the seller is unaware of the cup of coffee close.

Pre-empt the situation with the cup of coffee close. If it feels good and the vibrations are positive, offer to leave the group on its own for ten minutes.

The manager has made his pitch or the salesperson his final presentation to a group of decision-making managers. It is the easiest thing in the world for the Chairman to thank the speaker for making the case so well, and say that the managers will give it serious thought and discussion. The meeting ends with no decision because the chairman actually does want to hear everyone's views before a decision is confirmed. If they decide against, they can tell the salesperson by phone or by letter, always easier than face to face.

Pre-empt the situation with the cup of coffee close. If it feels good and the vibrations are positive, offer to leave the group on its own for ten minutes. 'Look, it must be difficult for you to make a decision while I am here, I'll go and have a cup of coffee while you have a chat. I'll pop back in a few minutes.' Either they are going to agree to your suggestion – a buying sign – tell you it is not necessary for you to go – another buying sign – or they are going to say that it is not necessary for you to return and that they will get back to you in due course, probably a warning signal.

It's quite fun if they agree to your returning in a few minutes. If when you return everyone looks at you, you have got the order. If only the Chairman is looking at you and some people are having their own quiet discussion you can be sure you have more work to do or that you have lost.

Idea 44 – Don't get mugged by politicians

Probably the most disastrous closing presentation I ever made was to the sub-committee of the finance committee of a large local authority. Three companies were bidding to replace and expand a considerable amount of computer equipment.

I decided to take with me a very sales-oriented technician in case the IT manager, an officer who would also be there as an adviser to the committee, asked reasonable questions which were beyond me.

I also took along a senior sales manager, whom I had briefed carefully. He prepared a good script that I vetted. This was the man from Idea 41 who rather ominously warned me that he was a lousy presenter. I ignored this remark on two grounds. He was a very good communicator in meetings and sales calls, and I did not think it was possible to get a senior sales job without being at least competent on one's feet.

We opened with the sales manager, who froze and stumbled and stammered through the text we had agreed, managing at the same time to make it more or less impossible to understand.

You could feel as well as see the restlessness of the councillors, themselves obviously reasonable orators, and the embarrassment of the IT manager, who felt a little responsible for what he was putting his masters through.

The chairman was a most fair and calm person who kept the questioning to a minimum at that stage and we passed on to the next presentation. I gave a short history of our joint success in implementing computer systems with solid benefits to all concerned. I then passed on to the overview of our new proposal and tried to demonstrate our competitive advantages in terms of the agreed basis of decision.

By now I would not say we were a wow, but we had recovered to at least looking professional. In retrospect I should have asked for the order at that time. Or at least I should have asked what we still needed to do to get the order.

But I had brought the technician with me and he had prepared a short but quite interesting few words about a technical innovation that distinguished our offering from the competition's. I overcame my instincts and put him on.

All went well until the IT manager asked a question, which the techie handled quickly and well. He had to drop into some detail but it was short and sweet. A Labour councillor then asked another question which was at a high level. The technician misunderstood the level and proceeded into a detailed explanation that was much more than the questioner required.

The politicians at this stage finally got bored, and did what they do when they are bored – had a snipe at the opposing party. The snipe received a firm retort, followed by a shouted list of mistakes the ruling party had made in several years of office.

By now the conversation was a million miles away from the topic in question and I looked to the chairman to help us out. He tried manfully, but when politicians smell fear or blood they go for the jugular. The chairman lost control and pandemonium broke out. It was like Prime Minister's question time on a bad day.

Our closing opportunity ended in chaos and the association of ideas the committee had with my company was malevolence and boredom. Needless to say, we did not win the business.

The Five Greatest Sales Ideas for Remembering that There is Always a Way

Introduction

Despite the thesis of this book that you can learn how to sell, I was reminded by the suggestions and stories that salespeople sent to me that there are no hard and fast rules about selling. Popularly called 'lateral thinking', looking for a way forward is a particular strength of good salespeople even when the odds looked stacked against and when a conventional approach seems to be failing. These ideas are, of course, examples, but I hope they can encourage us salespeople to believe that the unexpected works and that there is always a way.

The final, extra idea reminds us that there is also always a way to make a gaffe. Selling is as much about looking for what might go wrong as it is about making things go right.

I am convinced that salespeople would be well advised to use some of the sales processes found in this book and others, but from time to time there is no doubt that the good ones throw away the process and concentrate on the selling.

Idea 45 – Remember there is always a way (1)

A company board is in distress that their new shampoo is not selling well, and call in a sales consultant. 'For $30,000 I can double your sales with one word.' 'OK. What is the word?' 'At the end of the instructions for use on the back of the bottle, add "Repeat".'

Idea 46 – Remember there is always a way (2)

A financial director of a company whose computer solutions were held responsible for many of the problems of the company decided to take drastic action. She called in the IT director first, fired him and then every manager and technical person in the IT organisation. She then called in the computer supplier, whom she held responsible for their share of the problems and told them that she was taking out a writ that day suing them for non-performance. It was her intention to sue for aggravated damages when, as seemed inevitable, the company was plunged into chaos by failing to run the payroll and pay their employees at the end of the week.

The supplier salesperson was advised by his legal department that the suits could well prove successful. He then went and produced a project plan for using contractors which, since the machine room was intact and all the documentation present, looked as though it might get the payroll out on time.

The FD gave the supplier the opportunity to implement the plan – she was bound to or her suit would fail. Most people would have stopped there and got on with the job, but the salesman realised that the boot was moving to the other foot and insisted on getting an indemnity for previous failures signed before any contractors went on site. The FD again had to agree and the supplier not only saved the day but also landed a lucrative contract to manage the company's whole computer facility into the future. This was cheaper than having her own computer department and everyone was happy.

Idea 47 – Remember there is always a way (3)

The same salesperson lost a big contract for personal computers from a large organisation to a rival systems integration company. Since he knew the salesperson that had landed the deal he rang him to congratulate him. Finding that he had not yet placed the order for the sub-contractor who was going to provide the PC hardware he put in a proposal and got the order – same opportunity but a different customer.

Idea 48 – Remember there is always a way (4)

I had a problem with a series of terminals that suffered very badly from the static generated from the computer room carpet. It was our problem and eventually we modified the terminals and removed the fault, but it was cheaper and quicker for both parties in the original deal for us to pay for the carpet to be changed.

Idea 49 – Remember there is always a way (5)

The managing director of a systems integrator desperately needed to meet the CEO of the newspaper empire that was his largest customer. It also happened that the same CEO through another chain of companies owned the systems integrator. Add to this that the CEO was Robert Maxwell and you can see there is a challenge here. Maxwell's office was vague about when such a meeting could take place and significant time was passing.

The MD took action. He attended an Anglo/American club dinner that Maxwell was addressing. (How he got invited to the dinner is another proof of the value of remembering that there is always a way.) After the speech our hero waylaid Maxwell in the corridor on his way out. He explained who he was and Maxwell replied that he knew who he was and had expected him to get in touch before.

With that endorsement the way to a proper meeting was clear and easy.

Idea 50 – Remember there is always a way to make a gaffe

An American director of a UK company was on the stomp talking to staff who had been through a difficult period. His objective was to improve morale by pointing out, amongst other things, how multi-national the company had recently become.

He used as a proof how many of the overseas territories were run by local managers as opposed to by UK expatriates. His view was that it represented a maturing of a multi-national when the head of the office in Cairo was an Egyptian and so forth.

This had gone down quite well in London, Manchester and Leeds before the man got to the Scottish office in Edinburgh. He made the presentation and invited comments. Since the senior manager in Scotland was an Englishman at the time, the first question from the floor was inevitable. 'In view of the policy of appointing locals to run territories outside the home country, is it your intention to extend this privilege to Scotland?' The American director took a number of times to understand the question at all. He was making no distinction between Scotland and England, and he paid the price.

The Four Greatest Sales Ideas for Selling in a Small Retail Outlet

Introduction

One of the interesting things that happens when you become a freelance or set up your own business is that other people, particularly those involved in the selling side of business, frequently confide in you their version of the business of their dreams. Often they are doing just that – dreaming – and have no intention of attempting to make it come true. (Indeed, some people are on the brink of taking the plunge for so long that one comes to the conclusion that they are super-glued to the diving board.)

Sometimes their idea, if they were to implement it, would in fact be a nightmare. (I mean, have you ever really thought through what it would be like to run a pub in the country? It would be like opening up your living room to the same people every night whether you like them or not. And there are no police and no brewery overlord to enforce the licensing laws, so these people will stay until they want to go. Oh, and your hours are nine in the morning until, say, midnight, and that's on a good day.)

Nonetheless, there are good opportunities for turning selling skills into a business. In this section we are going to take as an example the business that most aspirant salespeople think about – retailing or consulting about things that excite them. So, if you want to open your art gallery or antiques shop, or if your bent is towards designing and installing kitchens or gardens, here are a few great ideas supplied by people who have done it and sold enough to achieve a lifestyle that suited them with an income sufficient to support it and more than a glimmer of hope that it might, with the Chancellor's blessing, turn into a retirement pension vehicle as well.

Idea 51 – Treat your customers as what they are – your purpose in life

Your customers are the agents who will fulfil your hopes. In the early stages you will have to spend a high proportion of your available cash on marketing. The guy who runs the art gallery told me: 'Spend 10% of each year's revenues on marketing, at least to begin with.'

Your stationary and your logo are important. Spend time and, if necessary, money on them.

Your stationary and your logo are important. Spend time and, if necessary, money on them. Your business name should have the echo of a branding or a positioning. It should suggest almost that new customers have heard of you before. This is not 'passing off', which is illegal, but making sure that the associations that people have with the name are positive and relevant.

You are always looking for repeat business and references to new prospects. If you can sell your product off the Internet, do it. This means that customers who were in your locale once can buy from you from wherever in the world they find themselves. Advertise in places where potential customers might come from. Remember, people with an interest in your speciality will travel to meet with and deal with someone who knows what they are talking about. So don't limit your advertising to your local paper. If your real pleasure comes from the buying of the products, don't let that diminish the amount of time you spend on promoting the business and finding new customers.

Once you have found them, keep a detailed record of who they are and what their interests are as well as what they bought. You will be surprised how quickly you build a database of information that makes your next mailshot extremely well focused – 'One of those tiny Georgian teapots has come into my possession, shall I keep it for the next time you drop in?' This database is a major asset of the business, and if you are eventually going to sell the business as a going concern it will be a huge contributor to the value of the goodwill you have built up.

Talking about goodwill, it is hard to win, but terribly easy to throw away. A good reputation pays huge dividends in terms of repeat business and new customers attracted by word of mouth. Set your quality sights very high. If a customer has a problem with a product, or even if they just don't like it, take it back or fix the problem, literally without question. Try, obviously, to get them to take something in exchange, but if they insist just give them their money back. It is quality and service you are selling, not the product itself. Use the best materials for display and packaging and make the place look welcoming. Your customers are used to being treated as people in a line, or as targets for smooth salespeople; shopping with you should be a different sort of experience. The opposite of pressure and intimidation is to leave them alone unless they ask for help and to go away when you have answered their question and they look as though they are going to move on to another product or even another shop. Remember, you are in this for the long haul; they will probably come back if they felt no pressure. Oh, and leave the door open whenever the weather allows it. This avoids any feeling of being trapped.

Talking about goodwill, it is hard to win, but terribly easy to throw away. A good reputation pays huge dividends in terms of repeat business and new customers attracted by word of mouth.

The shop will obviously change slowly as you sell items and bring in new stock, but a consensus of opinion says that you should make a point of changing the place dramatically from time to time. One person who sells rare books told me that it was his practice to start a collection of new offerings but keep them in a bottom drawer until he had a good display. This meant that he was possibly not selling the books as soon as he could, but it also meant that he could send out a mailshot inviting customers to come in and see the new display when the time came. He did this when the shop was otherwise closed, gave them a glass of wine and frequently did well.

One other person who sells a small number of quite highly priced goods made sure that on the counter there were a number of attractive but inexpensive related items, in this case postcards of well known paintings. This meant that everyone could buy something and was also a useful source of petty cash.

Idea 52 – Count your customers

Every sale you make, every business card you receive should be part of your customer database. Build it from the start and you will quite quickly and forever have the most precious marketing tool of the lot – people who have an interest in your products, and know you or your business.

The owner of the art shop explained it like this.

We started by collecting the Christmas card lists from all our friends on the basis that like attracts like. We added relevant people from my past business life, my wife's life as a teacher and entered all of these, about 550 records, into the Microsoft Word database. This is not ideal but what do you want – it's free if you have Word. This we called our prospect file. We then opened a visitor's book in the shop itself and encouraged people to sign it or throw their business card into a large, and quite attractive, glass jar. This added to the prospects file.

As we sold things and got customers we entered the details of the sale into an Excel spreadsheet that we call our customer file. Once again, not brilliant software but it seems fit for purpose and we will not change until we discover a major deficiency in it. We want to have the customers identified so that we can invite them to previews or for a glass of wine if we have something interesting to show them. It is also useful to be able to scan the file and see who is buying what.

We have stopped trying to guess exactly who will become customers because we still get so many surprises. All that means is that you must never throw any name away. Currently we have 1000 people on our prospect file and 500 customers. Combined with a good web page to which we can refer them from time to time, these give us a lot of our sales.

Idea 53 – Diversify carefully

Once you have your premises it is tempting to put them to greater use than just your original idea. There will, in fact, be no shortage of people offering to let you sell their wares through your shop for a percentage. Make sure that the wooden replicas hand-turned at a local crafts factory do not include a Trojan horse. Here is one good reason for looking at diversification with a sceptical eye – you really ought to learn as much about the new products as the old. After all, that is what you sell. There are other reasons:

- You must compare the use of the shelf space. Would it not make more sense to increase the stock of your main line of business? Granted that costs money, and they will let you display their toys for free, but that is what you are in business to do; buy more stock or stock of higher value. Besides, whatever the deal you do with your new supplier, it is bound to cost money in some way, and they will want their cash immediately you have sold something.
- The likelihood is that the product you are selling on behalf of somebody else is a simpler, lower price sale. Might not the time taken to make such sales detract from the time available to speak to potential customers of your main business? If it does then you have a resource problem. You need more staff in the shop, and you cannot get them in packages of less than one. If you only need a half a one, you are paying for an awful lot of magazine reading time.
- If you solve the staff problem by allowing the new supplier to be in charge from time to time, you hit the problem already discussed – they cannot sell your product because you are the product and you are not there.

The message from the front line is clear. Stick with what you know and make your own selling work. Don't get involved in someone else's.

Idea 54 – First run a pilot

If you are going to sell a new line or go nationwide with an idea, think of some way that you can test the water with a pilot before rolling it out to a full implementation.

In managing any project that involves change, most project managers find it advisable to run a pilot. This is good advice for the small retailer as well. As an entrepreneur you can do this with entire businesses. A good example of this is the high tech one where you create a new business with the minimum resources possible, a manager and a tightly knit team. In the team are, say, a couple of salespeople, a technical guru and someone for customer administration and support. This team then runs the micro business pretty much as though it were their own. They identify and sort out the problems, make it a success and teach you how the model works. You can then roll it out knowing the viability of the model and the financials. The technique is also brilliant for giving confidence to investors if you need them for the roll-out.

The Six Greatest Sales Ideas for Dealing with Difficult Products and Markets

Introduction

Selling, particularly selling new products, can be very hard. For example, if people find it difficult to understand your proposition because it is so new, you go through nightmares of wondering if it will ever sell. Most of the ideas in this book offer positive actions that you can take to push sales along and which have a track record of success. I think we can also learn from successful products that have been sold, sometimes over many, many years, and yet which have either no merit whatever or stretch a buyer's credibility to the very limit but still get the order.

So one of the ways to deal with sleepless nights caused by poor sales performance is to remind ourselves that somehow salespeople have managed to metaphorically sell sand to the Arabs or fridges to the Eskimos.

Idea 55 – Use physical attractiveness to sell rubbish

This is the only way that I can begin to explain the success of Madonna. Rod Liddle described her product in the Guardian on 7 May 2003 as 'some of the most gutless, vapid and anodyne "disco" music the world has ever heard.' I could not agree more, and when you are pacing during the witching hours it is helpful to remember that she sold millions of copies of this vapid rubbish. Go on, your product cannot be that bad.

Idea 56 – If at first it succeeds, sell it again and again

Religion is without any doubt one of the greatest business ideas of all time, as we agreed in the introduction to this book. Once again, to remind ourselves that someone can sell anything, it is extraordinary to remember that the current Christian church has beliefs and traditions that echo exactly the same concepts, miracles and wonders of religions that go back thousands of years. In fact, creationist Christians – they are the ones that believe that Genesis should be taken literally when it says that God made the world in seven days – believe that the world is only four thousand years old, and yet believe in concepts that science tells us were in wide use before that time – a nice irony.

The winter solstice is the shortest day of the year and in ancient times pagans celebrated the day as a rebirth of the sun god. The winter solstice was also seen as the birthday of a saviour man-god – the offspring of a god father and a human mother who was, of course, often a virgin. Here, according to August Berkshire in a paper *The Winter Solstice & Christmas* are just some: Tammuz of Babylon; Attis of Phrygia; Horus of Egypt; Mithra of Persia; Krishna of India; Heracles of Greece and Jesus of Nazareth. All these man-gods had their births celebrated at the winter solstice. How can people still buy it and believe that they are worshipping the true God made man? I bet your product is not so far-fetched.

Idea 57 – Obey the rules of supply and demand

Normal consumers deal with the phenomenon of supply and demand at, among other times, the time they buy or sell a property. For most people this is the most expensive asset they ever buy and it is hard to overestimate its importance to all of us. It can be a grisly business, with normally sensible and pleasant people finding the urge to scheme and lie to get the deal at the best possible price.

What is the value of your house? You can, of course, get an estimate from professionals in the business who base their guesses on properties in similar areas that have sold recently. But in the end the true market value is that which you are irrevocably offered by an exchange of contracts. Until then, the market, for example the person who is offering to buy your house, can change their bid up or down according to their view of the risk of making or breaking the deal. Once contracts are signed the true price, or market value, is established. But the following day that transaction is history and no one can be quite sure how the laws of supply and demand settle a new market value.

'You can't buck the markets' was a slogan made famous by Margaret Thatcher, the Prime Minister of the UK for the eighties and much of the nineties. And yet, argues Stelios Haji-Ioannou, business people continue to do so. This man, after revolutionising air travel by offering no frills cheap airfares, moved into various other areas and is poised at the time of writing to go into the cinema business. *His argument is simple but compelling – how can a seat in the cinema on a Monday afternoon have the same price as a seat in the same cinema to see the same film on a Saturday afternoon, when the demand for it is much more?* Using the Internet as the ticket distribution method, Easycinema will start tickets for the slow times of the week at as little as 20 pence. By doing this he hopes to increase the usage of each cinema seat from current performance, which can be as low as 50 per cent, to a much higher figure and make the current market much larger. He has a battle against the major film distributors to win, but as I said, the argument is compelling – obey the rules of supply and demand in order to sell those less desired products. After all, you would not put a property with a rough value of £250,000 on sale for £1,000,000 unless you were prepared for a lengthy wait for a buyer.

Idea 58 – Use television to cash in on fear

The evangelists in America use television to bring money pouring in, using their simple unique selling proposition, 'If you support us, we will support you in your bid to achieve immortality.' As long, says Pat Buchanan in his eerie way, as you are not a homosexual or come from Scotland, which he describes as a 'dark land'. Where did he get that from?

Idea 59 – Look out for different cultures

I can only raise the spectre of cultural pitfalls in this book; it could easily be another 100 Greatest Ideas title.

ABC – Always be closing

Publisher please note.

A friend of mine sold equipment to companies in Saudi Arabia. In this context 'companies' really means the Government. The equipment had done a fine job and there was only one matter outstanding – no one had paid the bill. A UK manager was sent out to collect the dues. When he got there he was met with civility, entertainment in the best hotels and sightseeing tours, but not with any money. Eventually he had to reach for the nuclear button and threatened to switch the machine off if the cheque was not in his hands within 24 hours.

The reaction was complete shock; how dare he make such a threat? However, they paid up and the manager went home. The relationship was never the same again.

In the same country I have had a similar experience. I was hired to run, amongst other things, a two-day training course. In the event the customer decided he wanted an extra day. I, of course, told him that would cost extra and again he was shocked. We had done a deal and he could not go back to his bosses and ask for more money.

I don't know if I will recover the situation since I am going to go and run the event, in two days of course, after I have finished this book.

Idea 60 – Don't make people want their own back

Selling difficult products or working in difficult markets does lead to strain on the relationship between supplier and customer. As a salesperson you are well aware that if customers make you feel bad by acting unreasonably you will plot how to get back at them and right the wrong. (In Idea 59 I could have given away the third day free; and taken it out of them in the next contract.)

Customers feel the same way. If they feel ripped off once and forced to take an action against their will or buy something that is less than they want, they will remember and probably manoeuvre a situation where you are the loser next time.

The Seven Greatest Sales Tips for Salespeople

Introduction

Most sports coaches and commentators spend a lot of time talking about and criticising sports players for their lack of attention to the basics. The same goes for selling. As I have been brought into sales situations, I am always impressed by how often it is quite easy to point to a basic flaw in the planning of the sales or marketing campaign – nothing complex, just the basics. A colleague of mine has met many sales teams planning how to handle an important account and how to close the complex sales situations they have on the go. He believes that he can predict what needs to go into the plan before he starts the session. Not only that, but he can predict what will need to be replanned and re-addressed when he returns for the three month update.

This is probably a little cynical, but getting the basics right will improve sales performance of all but the most meticulous salesperson. Here are some good ideas from seasoned salespeople.

Idea 61 – Learn to read upside down

The letterheads of your competitors, notes from advisers to managers, even entire sales proposals from your competitors are often on the desk of the person you are talking to. All you need to be able to do is read them upside down. 'Don't get too engrossed in the small print,' advises a person in the advertising business, 'Or you'll get rumbled. If this happens and the client quietly covers up the document you may still be OK. But if it is brusquely reversed so that you can read it properly you've probably lost.'

Idea 62 – Learn to read from the side

Similar to Idea 61, you will frequently be sitting beside someone with information you could use. This happened to me when I was on a plane going to a meeting to try to close a deal. The person in the next seat was reading the report that pertained to the solution I was trying to sell. Not only that but it had the numbers that all the competitors were in at. We were preferred but were not much more expensive. This forewarning enabled me to get the business without any further discount. It cost the company I was selling to some money and I had sore eyes for the afternoon.

Time is a great problem for a salesperson and the customer knows it. You have time targets to meet that are probably much more pressing than their need for your product or service.

Idea 63 – Don't fall for the 'We'll book your air ticket' ploy

This is a technique used by business people who are buying from overseas companies in particular. The people I have found who use it most are the Japanese. You go over there for three days to close a deal and find yourself really well looked after and entertained for the first two days. They then start the third day by offering to confirm your air ticket with the airline and with your office. Never let them do this. They then know exactly when you want the thing to be over and will leave a number of late hits that will cost you dear as you see the clock ticking towards your departure time.

The trick in this specific case is to decline their offer whenever it is made, explain that you have cleared your diary for as long as it takes and have a very flexible ticket. Never show them it. If you can, and this is particularly difficult in Japan, avoid the entertainment and dinners with senior people. Ask them rather if this could be left until after the business is settled and then you can have a celebration.

There is a broader issue here. Time is a great problem for a salesperson and the customer knows it. You have time targets to meet that are probably much more pressing than their need for your product or service. As Shakespeare put it, 'Screw your courage to the sticking place' and never let the customer see the pressure you are under to close the deal.

Idea 64 – Make your customer want to solve your problem

Just to show that there are no golden rules in selling but only solid guidelines with exceptions, this idea is exactly the opposite of Idea 63. If you have a good relationship with your customer it can often make sense to let them know exactly what you are required to achieve to meet your targets, by value and timescale. If the relationship is strong enough they may very well add these targets into their plan. After all, they want you to be successful and to have good leverage with your company so that they get top class service.

Idea 65 – Don't overplan

There is a syndrome in selling that many rookies suffer from. It is called by many 'analysis paralysis' and consists of salespeople taking too seriously the need to plan their activities, understand their customers and, for example, have a passing knowledge of their competitors. Taken too far it will save on shoe leather, but never get the salesperson out on the road. You will never have enough information; so get stuck in to the selling before paralysis takes place.

There is a good story of an ex-soldier who became a sales manager. This man was obsessed with maps. He occupied his first week by covering one complete wall of his office with a huge map of the British Isles. Using a special pencil he meticulously divided the realm into sales regions.

Then he stuck multi-coloured pins all over it – a cluster of white (so they stood out) for the main works and Head Office, another white for the London Office. He added two more for Regional Offices, red pins for sales reps and blue pins for customers. There was more – green pins for distribution depots, yellow pins for suppliers and purple pins for competitors. And, of course, they had to be reviewed and updated on a twice-weekly basis.

His boss, seeing the actual sales performance graph in bad decline, halted the analysis paralysis by suggesting that the manager took the pins off the wall and stuck them in the rear ends of his salespeople.

Idea 66 – People buy from people

People have often said that they do not care if the customer, internal or external, likes them or dislikes them, as long as they respect them. Maybe so, but in the end people buy from people, not from organisations, whether they have the utmost respect for them or not. In my view having your customer disliking you is likely to be a temporary situation – either they will change suppliers or your organisation will change you. The whole selling job becomes much easier when both parties like and respect each other. That way, both sides will take the rough with the smooth.

Idea 67 – 'It's about the customer, stupid'

My daughter is a sucker for another simple but frequently ignored technique – simple good customer service. Her best illustration is in a shop. If someone makes a real effort for her, tries to understand what she wants without making her mind up for her, she finds it difficult not to buy something. Once again, this is the transfer of need from satisfying the customer to satisfying the salesperson. Actually, it's not just my daughter, most good salespeople find it hard to say no to a decent seller. When we go out to tender for some electrical or building work, I find it really hard not to buy from the person who put most energy and thought into their solution. I also find it hard to tell anyone they lost. There is a big message in here somewhere – but it does come down to customer service.

The Six Greatest Sales Ideas for Planning a Complex Sale

Introduction – objectives and organisation of a campaign plan

First, the objectives of planning for complex sales:

- to agree the starting point from the prospect's point of view
- to agree the starting situation of the selling organisation
- to agree the overall objective(s) of the campaign
- to set milestones on the way to the objective in order to be able to monitor the implementation of the plan
- to identify the resources required to implement the plan and win the business
- to produce a detailed list of actions required to win the business
- to identify skills deficiencies in the sales team
- to get the team's and management's complete buy-in to the action plans and resource plan.

The process this section describes is relevant for any sales campaign that can be said to be complex; that is, one where there are a number of people involved in the buying process and a team involved in selling.

Having decided that on the face of it the campaign is about business which we want and which we can win, we can start to organize the process.

Idea 68 – Get the timing right

It is of little value to call the team together before the customer has reached, either with you or without you, that part of the buying cycle that identifies the objective of some putative investment.

Experience shows that the right time to do the original plan is when the customer is at least some way through the buying cycle but some significant time away from the decision on suppliers.

You can be too late as well. To pull the team together just as the customer is about to make a decision also leads to a less productive planning session. There is frankly little that can be done to influence the way the campaign is going, and the team will simply produce a situation report which will record the fact that they are likely to win or likely to lose. The best test for the right time to get into the process is whether or not the selling team can produce a meaningful campaign goal. The team needs to be able to state what they are going to try to sell and what overall benefit the customer is going to gain.

Experience shows that the right time to do the original plan is when the customer is at least some way through the buying cycle but some significant time away from the decision on suppliers. If we take a lengthy buying cycle then probably we should consider the right time to be when the customer is at least three months from a decision date but not more than nine months away. These matters are complicated by customers frequently being unable to put down and stick to a decision date, but common sense should tell us when we need to get the team together.

Idea 69 – Set a stretching campaign goal

Getting this first step right is a vital part of the planning process. It enables the team to focus their efforts on an agreed aim and allows them to check with the customer that he or she is reading the situation correctly.

As with all objective setting which we will deal with in this book, a campaign goal must obey the rules. Remember that to be an acceptable statement of the team's aim a goal must be SMART (see Idea 5):

- **S**tretching
- **M**easurable
- **A**chievable
- **R**elated to the customer
- **T**ime-targeted.

Idea 70 – Check sales campaign goals with the customer

Some salespeople are uncomfortable with the prospect of showing the customer the basis for a sales campaign. They worry that the customer will baulk at a price given too early, or a timescale with which he or she cannot at this stage agree.

I do not understand the logic of this. In solution selling we are always trying to understand why the customer will not buy as well as why he will. The earlier we know about any objection in the mind of the customer, the better we can make our plan to deal with it.

A simple trial close can give good return and add to the plan significantly.

- Seller: 'We are aiming to supply the solution for completion of the installation by the end of July.'
- Buyer: 'No way. There will be a bottleneck on the engineering effort required which makes that date far too optimistic.'
- Seller: 'If we could show you an implementation plan which identifies those engineering resources and gets implementation complete by July, would you consider it?'

The vigour with which the customer sustains this objection will tell the seller how feasible is the earlier date. In any case, the discussion of the campaign goal has started the process well by identifying the concerns of the customer that, if not dealt with, will become objections to the sale.

Idea 71 – Use a structured campaign planning process

Stages in a planning process

In a complex campaign, environmental analysis concerns the customer's buying cycle, the customer's reasons for buying and our qualification of the project. Qualifying the prospect deals with whether we can win the business and whether the profit available is worth the effort we will have to put in. The process can be expressed as a flow diagram (see figure).

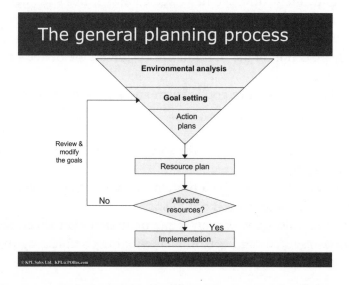

The shape of the chart is driven by experience that has identified that if it takes one unit of time, an hour or a day, say, to set the milestones for the campaign, it takes two units to analyse the environment and half a unit to decide on the action plan.

When it comes to setting milestones for our progress in the sale, they are best divided into two types: the customer's business issues and our people issues. In this way we are pursuing both the logic of the sale, i.e. what is in it for the customer, but also the psychological and people issues which are the focus of the skill of selling.

Both areas are essential. If we do not assist the customer to prove his business case, someone else may and if that someone else is a competitor then he will be gaining competitive advantage.

Besides, if there is no real financial and strategic reason for the customer to buy, someone in the organisation is going to call a halt. This person is frequently quite high in the company and the damage done is more than wasted selling effort, it is also the loss of reputation with an influential person. Their first impression of the selling company is that it pursues sales for their own exclusive benefit rather than checking that there is something in it for the customer as well.

The key to getting the activity plans practical is accountability.

Another problem the inevitable delay of a poor business case causes the supplier is an internal one. They probably twisted arms and struggled to ensure the availability of the resources to do the next step. The embarrassment of delay will also turn into a loss of credibility the next time that wants resource.

A project is frequently delayed because of the lack of a good business case for the customer. But the people issues are equally important. Once the selling team can see what it needs to achieve to win the business, it can start the activity plans. The key to getting the activity plans practical is accountability. Each action must have an owner who has accepted the job and the timescale for it.

Remember that only people involved in the creation of the plan can be assigned actions. If other resources are required to make a contribution, then a member of the planning team is given the action to liaise with the managers of those resources and get their agreement to the action and the timescale.

Resource planning and the management review process

Any planning process ends up with a number of goals or milestones and a series of actions the team is committed to take to achieve these aims. Resource planning should be a simple resort of the activities by resource.

The team knows what results they are striving for and have established what they need to do. They are now in a position to inform management of the plan. They take their resource plan to the managers responsible for the required resources of people, machinery and money. A decision is made.

This is a crucial time in the life of the plan. When the selling team makes its presentation both sides, management and the team, must be clear whether the review is to look at the quality of the plan or whether it is to commit resources to the implementation.

Management will have lots of submissions to look at. If they are at the stage of the financial year where they are reviewing plans all round the organisation before making decisions on resources, they must make this absolutely clear to the teams.

Let us assume that both management and the team are certain that a review meeting is going to make decisions on resources. Lots can still go wrong, particularly in an organisation which is in the throes of putting formal planning into its selling teams.

The best way to approach the meeting is in terms of a contract. The selling team proposes the result they believe they can achieve, normally measured by sales revenues, as we have said, and/or profit. They also produce the resource plan which they believe is required if the goal is to be achieved. It is management's prerogative to question and suggest change to the action plans and therefore resource plans. They are in a position to suggest work which has been done elsewhere and which could offer the selling team some shortcuts.

Very significantly, they are in a position to know whether or not the resources requested have the necessary knowledge, skills and experience to carry out the actions assigned to them. This too can change or in extreme cases invalidate the plan.

In the end the agreement is made and the contract accepted. 'We will give this result if you will give us these resources.' There is an important point still to be remembered by both sides. All contracts, particularly stretching contracts, are taken in good faith with 'best intentions' on both sides.

Sometimes one or other of the parties will fail. Just as the selling team can give no guarantees of success in a competitive world, so management will sometimes fail in its endeavours to provide the promised resource. A missed deadline on a product improvement, for example, is going to occur. The key is for both sides to recognize and acknowledge the risks.

The whole thing can go hopelessly wrong if the company culture becomes one of less than openness by either or both parties.

If the selling teams get the impression that any proposal they make is going to be accepted as good by management, but that they will then require the team to achieve it with much less resource than is in the plan, then the selling team will add a little to the resource plan, knowing that it will be cut.

If the management team feels that any proposal the selling teams make will probably be less than can be achieved and take more resources than are actually required then a vicious circle starts. Worse still, opportunities will be lost where the selling team makes an assumption that the resources will not be available to exploit them.

In a mature planning organisation the results are stretching but achievable, the resources sensible and expected to work professionally. In such a case this initial review will produce an agreed contract that with best efforts will succeed. Further review will occur as time passes, the team makes progress and things change.

Idea 72 – Go through a structured campaign planning process step-by-step

By now the team has in mind a campaign goal and has agreed with an appropriate senior manager at the customer that it obeys the rule of being a SMART objective.

The team needs now to assemble the team to validate the goal and produce the campaign plan. In common with all business decisions there is always an element of the unknown. As you discover holes in your knowledge base, note them down in the plan. Then when you come to action planning you can put one of the team members in charge of collecting the missing facts.

How long the team should allow

This is a difficult question to answer. If the team is new to the process and the campaign goal is big enough to merit it, you should allow two days. This is sufficient time to do a thorough job on the environmental analysis, decide as a team the milestones involved in achieving the goal and agree an action plan. It is also enough time to prepare and carry out a management review, either to inform management of the plan or to obtain agreement to the resource plan.

Although in theory a team should continue with the process for as long as it takes for them to be satisfied with the quality of the work, in practice most teams need a time target. The prior agreement of a manager to attend a briefing at, say, 3.45 p.m. on the second day gives a useful focus to the event. The team is aware that they need to have something sensible to say before that time. The timescale for an audit of an existing plan is shorter, say a day or even a more regular half-day.

Prior to the event

Here is a checklist of what needs to be done before the campaign planning is started in earnest.

- *Get the agreement of the team members and their management that they are committed to attend:* Try to do this well in advance and confirm the arrangement in writing. Planning tends to demonstrate its benefits some time after it has been done. You always run the risk therefore that a crisis that can be solved in the short term gets a higher priority on the actual day of the planning event. The planning team should include anyone who will be involved in the implementation of the plan and take accountability for some of the actions.

- *Agree a time for an appropriate manager to come to hear the plan review:* The most appropriate manager is the one who has the authority to agree all the resources. This person may not be available because of the number of plans he or she would have to review, and a compromise may be necessary. It is certainly useful for the manager to have some control over some of the required resources.

- *Send out a briefing document to all team members:* Make sure that everyone is aware of the objectives of the planning event and of the putative campaign goal the salesperson is going to propose. Set their expectations for what the event will have as its output. Emphasize that it is not only a think-tank but also a decision-making forum where they are going to be asked to commit themselves to actions and accountability for their completion.

  Include in the briefing the minimum of information necessary for the team to be aware of the customer opportunity and have a passing knowledge of your company's relevant products and services. The event itself is not the appropriate time to go into great detail, particularly on technical issues, so keep it short and simple.

- *Agree the customer input:* Campaign plans are normally created without reference to the customers. After all, you are going to get into detailed areas of politics and people, yours and theirs. It is a shame, however, to miss the opportunity to impress customers with the professionalism of the process you are going to use. They will probably also be interested in the fact that you and your company are taking the campaign seriously.

  In this regard you may get further confirmation of how seriously the customer is approaching the matter. Few customer managers wilfully allow a supplier to go to the sort of trouble and expense of running a planning session unless there is some intention on their part to do something about the problem or opportunity. It is often therefore a good idea to invite the customer to make a contribution to the plan, perhaps as an after dinner speaker on the topic or during the event itself.

> *In order to sell into the heart of a company and its direction you need to understand how the project you are proposing fits into the company's strategy and direction.*

- *Choose a good location:* If it is possible, bring the technology with you to allow a member of the team or someone brought in especially for the task to produce the paper document at the end of the first day. This document is the hard copy of what the team has produced in flip chart form.

Idea 73 – Drive a campaign plan from an assessment of the customer's business issues

The first responsibility is to look at the customer requirement and ask searching questions about why the customer will buy from a business point of view.

What is the customer's business objective for this campaign?

In order to sell into the heart of a company and its direction you need to understand how the project you are proposing fits into the company's strategy and direction. Use this question to try to compose a single sentence that connects the project with a major company strategy or vision.

Getting the customer's business objective for the project right is important. It sets the theme of how you are going to interest and sell to every level of management in the organisation. It is also a very short-cut method of briefing anyone from the selling company on the overall reason why the customer is going to buy. If you have decided to involve the customer in your planning event, you may be able to agree this statement there and then.

What critical success factors declared by the customer does this campaign address?

Now broaden your search for how well the project fits the customer strategy. You need to understand from published material or from questioning the customer what issues are believed to be critical to the customer achieving his business objectives. These are frequently identified in the company's Annual Report. Starting from there you need to check again at the highest level possible whether the CSFs (critical success factors) are still current. Such a conversation will also give you other ideas for fitting the project to the customer strategy.

What benefits, both tangible and intangible, will the customer derive from a successful implementation?

This is a straightforward list of all the potential benefit areas. The list distinguishes tangible benefits from intangible. The difference is that tangible benefits can be reduced to a sum of money whereas intangible benefits can be seen as useful but not quantifiable. Tangible benefits are much more persuasive to a board of directors than intangible.

What are the rough costs of all the expenditure involved?

Make a list of all the expenditure the customer will be involved in. This list needs to be comprehensive. Make sure that there are no hidden extras.

How does the prima facie return on investment case look?

Even at this stage you and the customer can make a first draft of the cost–benefit analysis. The main holes in the case are likely to be in estimating the tangible benefits. In the action plan which will follow you will put down activities such as meetings with line managers to gain their agreement to the quantification of the business case.

What key ratios will be the basis of how the customer measures the success of the project?

Directors and managers at all levels of a business have in their minds a number of key ratios. For example, first line sales managers will be aware at most times what their sales revenues are to date compared to where they should be at this time of the company year.

Solution selling demands that we understand what financial ratios each of the key people holds important. From that knowledge we can tailor the presentation of benefits to illustrate the impact on those ratios that are personally important. We will not always be successful, as no project can be expected to hit the hot buttons of every executive involved, but it is a good challenge to try to be as comprehensive as possible.

Where in terms of geography and company divisions will the benefits occur?

If the product you are selling is going to have a wide impact, it is necessary to make a good list of where the benefits must be sold. At some point you need a groundswell of opinion moving towards a recommendation for your product, and the wider and louder this groundswell is, the better the chances of success.

What are the risks the customer will take if it goes ahead with this project?

This is not the detailed risk analysis a company looks at in calculating return on investment, but more a strategic look at the risks involved. Use the strategy statements from above such as the company's objective for the project or the company's CSFs as a guide to this part of the exercise. Is this project, while consistent in theory with the buying company's strategy and CSFs, putting any of these areas at risk?

How does the size of this project compare with others the customer has undertaken?

The reason for this question is that it is part of the start of the selling company's qualification process. With the best will and business case in the world, companies remain fearful of the unknown or the new.

There is a big difference between examining the technical and financial case for putting in a huge new way of doing things, and taking the decision to do it. It is always easier to sell the second implementation than the first. Equally it is always more likely that a company will go ahead with a project if it has done something of similar size before.

If this is a bigger or more geographically spread venture than the customer has attempted before, the selling team needs to take that into account in planning the campaign. Very deliberate actions will be put in place to try to build up the confidence of the customer that the project implementation will be successful. Indeed, it may be very desirable to identify this risk in more detail. It is not unusual to suggest that the customer buys some consultancy services to look at contingent risks brought on by a project.

The Four Greatest Sales Ideas for Qualifying Out Proactively

Introduction

The most time that any salesperson wastes is working on sales that eventually come to nothing or go to the competition. That is why so many of the good ideas in this book concern planning, reviewing your position and qualifying the prospect hard through out the campaign.

It is a great mistake to think that qualifying out is a passive thing. After all, you only have to stop trying to make a sale and the prospect will get the idea that you are no longer interested. Perhaps the worst case I was on the receiving end of took place with an advertising space salesman, who came into my office and asked lots of questions about my business. At the end of a short meeting he left his notes about my needs on a table in the office while he put his coat on. We chatted on for a bit, then he departed, leaving his notes on the table. I obviously expected him to call and get me to send them to him, but having heard nothing for a few days I divined that he had qualified me out.

The active process of qualifying out does two very positive things. If you do indeed have no chance of getting the order it saves loads of time that you can spend on other campaigns where you have a better chance. You can also use it as a harsh test of whether a person you are selling to is ever going to convert into a buyer. These ideas reflect both of these outcomes.

Idea 74 – Use a very direct approach by asking a hard question

There are many versions of this and they frequently involve using your manager. Suppose you have been working on a deal for some time. You have been using your own and your company's resources trying to refine and demonstrate the benefits of your proposal. Try pushing the pressure back on to the customer by asking your manager to intervene with a very hard question.

This worked for a computer saleswoman who was under a lot of stress trying to get an order that she had been forecasting for a while and that had slipped month by month for nearly half a year. She got her sales manager to give her a strict instruction about the prospect, if you see what I mean. The sales manager agreed to do it and the salesperson was able to go to her prospect and truthfully say, 'My manager has instructed me to pull out of this deal. He will only reconsider this if your managing director gives my boss his personal assurance that you are serious about making a decision.' There are three possible outcomes to such a hard question:

- If the prospect is serious they will realise that they are simply putting the decision off, get their MD to give the assurance and move rapidly to a conclusion. (A variation on this move is where the salesperson is in collusion with the prospect's main recommender. They use the hard question so that the recommender makes certain that they are going to be allowed to spend the money.)
- The salesperson learns from the prospect that there is indeed no chance of an order in a sensible amount of time using a sensible amount of resource in this case. What happens is that the prospect refuses to ask for the MD's assurance or the MD refuses to give it. In either case you have got the message and can move on.
- The third outcome is similar; where the prospect refuses the assurance but challenges the salesperson by saying that whilst they cannot give such an assurance there is a very good chance that the order may come in the not too distant future.

Idea 75 – Ask a logical and serious business question

When I worked for a training organisation, I had one saleswoman who found it impossible to qualify out. Her prospect list never did anything but grow. She was taking orders, but I had a concern that she was operating on too broad a front. When I asked her to qualify some out, she looked at the list hard and then announced that they were all still valid prospects.

I persuaded her to let me ring the prospects as the manager of the resources who did the actual training when a sale was made. I asked each person on the list for an idea, not of when they would place the order, but of when I should tentatively allocate training resources to their company. This perfectly fair question had the effect of getting sensible answers from managers who did not want to waste my time. The result was a considerable amount of qualifying out and a much more focused saleswoman.

Idea 76 – Ask the prospect to do something

This idea is an excellent one where you have better interest from a senior manager than you have from a middle manager who may not be so keen on your proposal. Work out an activity that you need the middle manager to do. Make it straightforward enough not to be a ludicrous amount of time or energy, but difficult enough for them not to want to do it. Put it in writing.

Give them time to fail by not following up. After a suitable break, face the senior manager with the problem. Then you will find out if the senior manager is really trying to push your idea through, or if they are going to be stopped by middle management treacle and delay. You can use the same technique on a single person with no reference up the way.

Idea 77 – Use the 'obvious decision' ploy

If you feel you are not making good progress in a sale, you are probably right.

If you feel you are not making good progress in a sale, you are probably right. Test the water by working out what would be an alternative decision to your proposal that makes sense. Then call the prospect and challenge them, in the nicest possible way, with that conclusion.

When selling a computer solution to a local government region, I had a concern that they would be bound to choose a supplier who had a small manufacturing facility in their region. This meant that at least one councillor had the people who worked in that factory in his constituency. I phoned the Chief Executive and politely indicated that I had heard on the grapevine that it made sense that they would do this. The impact was dramatic. The CEO went ballistic and told me in no uncertain terms that they were making a business decision not a political one.

I got the business and still believe that the CEO wanted to go to another supplier than the home grown one to make a point.

The Three Greatest Sales Ideas for Closing the Deal Softly, Softly

Introduction

I talk about focusing your selling by closing all the time throughout this book. It is one of the top ideas chosen by all the people I talked to. It is quite hard, though. Continuous closing can get on peoples' nerves, and you do not want to be known as a nag or a bore. So, instead of continuously asking the closing question 'Can I have your order?' try these two softly, softly techniques. The third idea reminds us that there are no rules in selling. Any opportunity can arise to help us close business. Think laterally, oh – and ABC, always be closing, or alternatively trial closing. (Geddit?)

Idea 78 – Use the trial close

The trial close is a powerful ally, used much less in personal life than you might expect, since it is as useful with children as well as with prospects. It simply gives a condition and asks the closing question on that. 'If I could get it to you by Thursday, would you be in a position to give the go-ahead now?'

Use it to measure your progress and find out what you have to do to get the business. (Incidentally, the bold question – What do I have to do to get the business? – is pretty crude, and normally shows the asker to be in a position of weakness. If you are selling competitively it usually means that you think you are losing to someone else.)

Trial closing stops you doing things that were not entirely necessary. 'If we get someone to courier stock within two hours, would that make you feel happy to sign?' If this gets the answer, 'Well I hardly think we need to worry about that amount of time. Our system should place orders with less urgency than that,' you have saved a lot of money and trouble.

Finally, trial closing reminds your customer of why, in the end, you are there. It keeps the relationship cosy and as non-threatening as possible, without taking the risk that the customer wants your friendship more than your products.

Idea 79 – Use an alternative close

Another quite forceful but less frightening close is the alternative close. 'Are you thinking about the blue one or the red one?' It seems a bit crude in the retail environment, but in more complex environments it can be an excellent indicator of your progress. You cannot generalize about the actual words to use; you have to work out what subtle alternatives are available in your product or service and construct the words.

Idea 80 – Use the mouth of babes

Finding ways of leaking information to clients in a way that they do not think that you are the source of the leak is an old technique.

Finding ways of leaking information to clients in a way that they do not think that you are the source of the leak is an old technique. It uses a third party in some way to add credibility to your arguments. Other customers are very good for this. If you have a good enough relationship you can generally get them to say things that are very helpful to your case. Doing it when you are not there tends also to add credence.

I am not sure if the following is a good technique in this area or not, but it happened by chance and once again it worked.

A salesperson was coming towards the end of a difficult sales campaign. He got an unexpected, and therefore very welcome, call from the decision-maker in the client organisation asking him to pop in to clarify a few points. The only problem was that he was that day a househusband looking after his young son. He told the customer of the problem, who responded by telling him to bring the boy in.

The salesman gave the child strict instructions to keep quiet; but the customer insisted on welcoming his son and talking to him to put him at his ease. Eventually the little boy said the only thing that he knew about the prospective deal, which was that his dad had promised that he would take him out to a special lunch if he got the order.

What could the prospect do?

The Ten Greatest Ideas for Implementing Account Management

Introduction

To attain your aspirations as an account manager, you have to keep thinking and planning. The problem this gives you is how to build a bridge from your hopes to a creative plan where the output is what you and your team are actually going to do. Most successful people have found this out and arranged for themselves and their board and other teams of people to go off-site to produce a plan. For this you need a process – the creative planning process. All planning processes include three elements – analysis, objective setting and activity planning. This section illustrates this in a particular circumstance – building the account plan you need in order to maintain and expand your biggest customers. I use this one as an illustration because it has the element of analysing the customer position as well as your own. You can equally well, with only minor alterations, use the same process for building a creative business plan.

So it's not optional; get the people who need to be there together and build a creative plan.

Idea 81 – Of course we will always keep our biggest customers ... (not)

This idea and the next one are mainly concerned with the sellers of complex products developing their major customers by selling high quantities of products and services to large businesses with long chains of command. You may sell heating and ventilation systems to contractors, for example, or fast-moving consumer goods to supermarkets. Another contender for this treatment is consultancy, be it management consultancy or recruitment. The key is that you are a selling team, and that you are selling to a buying team. It is, of course, a logical extension of big ticket selling, but this is the joined-up version where you are active in a key account all the time, continuously taking orders from them and always in some way involved in delivering or implementing what you have sold.

Key account customers for many businesses supply 80% of the orders taken in any one year. The loss of any of them causes problems, the loss of the biggest or more than one of the others could be catastrophic. (BNFL claimed in 2000 to have some 30 customers and therefore to be secure even although they were losing all their Japanese business. The Japanese business just happened to put into the shade all the other customers put together.)

So we need a system or business process that monitors and ensures customer satisfaction and at the same time builds the overall relationship and finds new opportunities preferable before the competition.

It is easy to become too dependent on one customer.

The position of BNFL is not uncommon. It is easy to become too dependent on one customer. After all, it is much easier to make sales to people who know you, and finding a new prospect in the same organisation takes much less effort than finding a new customer altogether. And by definition the key account is pleased with you. Your business processes are in synchronisation, regular delivery means that your people and theirs are working in familiar areas and so on.

Indeed, some companies become too dependent on a small number of customers because the customer is delighted to assist in making this happen. Their negotiating position becomes better and better, whilst, although the short term may show larger profits, the supplying company's negotiating position is becoming worse and worse. Even if there is absolutely no malice aforethought, the world changes and a big company strategy that has worked for many years can suddenly go phut. Think about Marks & Spencer, who carried their buy-British strategy on for so long that their share price crashed and their leading directors left to spend more time with their families. The effect on those who depended too much on them was catastrophic.

As I said before, I cannot really find any scientific evidence for what constitutes becoming too dependent but a rule of thumb that I have used has been given a positive reception by the people I have discussed it with – don't get more than 33% of any year's revenue from a single account.

Idea 82 – Set a clear account planning mission

So you have a small number of key accounts and, let us say, are the account manager responsible for them. You need to get your team to produce a plan to ensure and exploit that long-term relationship. The 'bible' of the account manager is the key account plan, or whatever you choose to call it.

A planning session starts from a vision or mission. We want to change, possibly dramatically, a part of the world to our vision of it. The mission could be very broad or very focused; but it gives the starting point of the plan.

The objective of a planning session is 'To produce the best possible plan to achieve this mission'. Notice how the objective breaks the rules of normal objectives – 'best possible' is not an accurate measurement for achievement. We have to accept this, though, as a more accurate test for success could constrain the creative thinking of the plan.

Examples of planning team mission statements could look like this:

- to be the supplier of first choice to the account in all of Europe and North America
- to be and to be seen to be a major supplier in the Civil Government market
- to improve our market share in the account worldwide
- to achieve at least a 10% higher level of revenue growth in the account every year for the next three years
- to use our reputation in the pharmaceuticals division of the customer to gain 10% of the orders placed in the Chemicals division within a year.

Idea 83 – Get the logistics of account planning right

If a good planning session is worth its weight in gold, it is important to get the right people into the right place at the right time and for the right time.

Who is there?

The planning team should include most of the people who will be involved with the implementation of the plan. The account manager, any technical support person and possibly a marketing person may be appropriate.

If there is a facilitator, he or she will be responsible for describing and getting agreement to the ground rules of planning. He or she will also police and time the session to ensure that by the end the team has reached an appropriate point in the process.

It is highly desirable for you or another senior manager to attend the last session of the Key Account Planning event to hear a short presentation of the team's conclusions. This gives a focus to the team, who will have to be ready to make such a presentation when the time comes.

How long do you work?

If your plan is concerned with a limited part of the customer's business you should be able to put a plan together within a day. Bigger teams with bigger tasks could take a lot longer. By the way, experience shows that after eight or nine hours the productivity of planners drops dramatically. It is probably better, therefore, to finish at around 5.30 p.m. If it is a new team or some new members are joining, it is a good idea to have the meeting off-site and to have dinner together. Don't forget, though, you are trying to make these planning events regular and routine. It is a good idea to call a one or two day planning session to modify a particular part of the plan and to hold such a meeting in an ordinary conference room.

The documentation of a planning session should be on flip charts subsequently transferred to an electronic file.

Idea 84 – Use a creative account planning process

The word 'creative' reminds us that we are looking for the best possible plan. Try to avoid all your prejudices and preconceived ideas. In particular, in the early part of the planning process do not let your thinking be constrained by doubts about the availability of resources.

We will, of course, recognize that there is a management budgeting cycle and that each plan needs to have resources approved at appropriate times during that cycle.

Nevertheless, we need creative ideas to generate new initiatives. After all, any company's management can put resources where they like. If the team gives management a good business case and enough time to react you may have to buy in resources seeing from the plan the results that will follow.

The steps of the creative planning process are outlined below.

Gather a database of knowledge

Remember the Chinese proverb – do not decide where you want to go and how to get there until you are quite certain where you are now.

The team needs to understand the customer's business, the customer's industry, the customer's current financial and competitive environment, the influences of the general economy etc.

That's before the team adds the supplier company environment, its current market strategies, position in the account, products and services etc. If we have organized a huge database of knowledge, planning will become more and more effective.

For the moment let us imagine that either before or during the event the account manager has briefed the planning team on the information necessary to take part in the creation of the plan.

In a new account penetration plan there will be little information to hand and the planning session will be quite short. But the more information available to the team, the better.

The team will never have all the facts at its fingertips. Indeed, in a new account penetration plan there will be little information to hand and the planning session will be quite short. But the more information available to the team, the better.

Soft data is in many ways as important or even more important than hard data. It includes all the prejudices and politics of the people side of the business. This data consists of the subjective opinions drawn by customer managers or the account team.

Do not take things at face value – in any large company there is an organisation chart. It is hard data. It says: 'That person reports to that person, who reports to that person, who reports to that person etc.'

The soft data asks: 'Yes, but who actually runs the business, who has influence, who can make things happen and equally – who can stop things happening?'

In many large British companies there is a network of people with similar backgrounds who, though in different divisions and at different levels in the business, form a powerful virtual team.

In one very large privatised business the organisation chart did not reveal – without further examination – the fact that many established and up and coming executives had not only attended the same university, but also the same college.

The environment section of a creative planning process includes the background knowledge, including the soft data brought by everyone in the team.

Analyse this data

The analysis technique for sorting out your knowledge and different team members' angles on the plan is called SWOT analysis – Strengths, Weaknesses, Opportunities and Threats.

This is a simple technique, as so many good ones are, for helping the team to understand what it needs to do in the account.

Unfortunately, like all techniques it can be implemented well – and badly. Suffice it to say that a comprehensive, well-documented SWOT analysis makes the next part of the planning process reasonably straightforward.

The objective of SWOT analysis is not simply to describe the environment; rather it is to describe the environment in a way that helps us to understand what we need to do.

It is in two parts, the customer SWOT (C-SWOT) and the supplier SWOT (S-SWOT).

Once you have got an agreed description of the environment you can decide what to do about it.

Set the objectives for the team

Following the use of a bridging technique to ensure that the work done in the SWOT analysis is fully exploited, the team sets its goals.

In a key account plan goals are divided into account management goals and sales campaign goals.

Account management goals are the relationship goals and tend to be more strategic and longer term than campaign goals. Experience has enabled professional account managers to break down account management goals into eight goal areas.

Not all plans will require goals in all eight areas but all plans will require goals in some of these areas. The detail of this follows, but for the sake of example, three of these goal areas are:

- level of contact
- customer satisfaction
- market share.

Campaign goals are goals where a major milestone is taking an order from a customer for the supplier's products and/or services. The methods used for campaign planning are explained in Ideas 68–73.

Having decided what we want to achieve, you get to the last part of the planning process – the activity plans.

Plan the activities necessary to achieve the objectives

It is very much a personal decision as to the amount of detail into which activity plans have to go.

It is very much a personal decision as to the amount of detail into which activity plans have to go. Some people are comfortable with quite macro actions and milestones that are weeks or even months apart. Other people try to plan all the activities required to achieve the objective in the minutest detail, even down to a telephone call.

It is personal preference. Either will do as long as it achieves the aim of activity planning, which is to estimate the resources required to achieve the objective.

The team should now be in a position to produce its best forecast of its achievements in the account both short-term and long-term and the amount of resource investment required from the supplying company to achieve these results.

Re-sort the activity plan into a resource plan

The resource plan is actually a re-sort of the activity plan. If you know what has to be done and who has to do it you can produce your best estimate of the resources required.

This enables us to move to the next step in the planning process. This is either part of the normal budgeting cycle or on some occasions a special case to take to management as a long- or short-term business investment plan.

It is vital to narrow down an accurate definition of the resources that will implement the plan. Too often the team starts to implement the early part of the plan, only to find a resource problem later.

The team needs to get itself into good order to move to the next step, which is to persuade management to put those resources at the team's disposal.

Idea 85 – Get agreement to the allocation of the resources to implement an account plan

Most account plans require resources not in the direct control of the account team. A decision box therefore occurs when management decide on the merits of the various plans being put forward and allocate their resources.

Try to see this as a contract. The account team is saying to management: 'I will give you these results' – meaning the objectives – 'if you will give me these resources.' If management say yes, either immediately or as the budgeting cycle grinds on, the team implements the plan.

If management say no, the team adjusts its goals and resubmits, because, of course, no planning process is complete until the resources have been allocated to its implementation.

Be careful. Management can often from their wider experience offer short-cuts towards account teams' objectives and therefore legitimately reduce the amount of resource required to achieve the result.

However, in an immature planning cycle, management, particularly sales management, have a habit of liking the sound of the result, but not allocating the resource in full.

At worst this leads to teams second-guessing the likelihood of their getting resources when they are setting goals and completely constrains the creativity of the plan.

For their part, account teams must recognize that while management can get any resource required to achieve a well-constructed business plan, it requires more than a week's notice. The plans must signal in detail this year's resource requirement and broadly the requirement of the subsequent two years, particularly if special or unusual resources are going to be required.

Idea 86 – Get the team to toe the line

Any planning team needs to obey some ground rules concerned with the efficiency of the planning session. Where two or three people are gathered together you will find differences of opinion, multiple ideas, different angles on the same topic, personal prejudices and all the other features of a team of human beings.

These tend to reduce the efficiency of a team. It is the job of the facilitator, and of course of the team itself, to maintain a number of disciplines.

1   *Talk and document in short, simple but complete sentences:* This item is proved in the detail on SWOT analysis, and is probably the most important rule. If we talk in bullet points then we will get quick agreement to a rough definition of the key issues. But, what we need is the agreement of the team to a detailed statement of the *real meaning* of the key issue.

2 *Equal voice/equal vote:* In a creative planning session, rank disappears. It is vital that the planning team does not believe that it is there to wait until the senior person has expressed a view and then agree with it.

Real creativity may easily come from a member of the team who is the most junior and therefore the least experienced. So, chief executives and account managers, a sure way to kill the creativity of your team is to make it plain, after about an hour of planning, that the only plan which is going to be acceptable is the one you had in your head before the meeting started.

In a creative planning session, rank disappears. It is vital that the planning team does not believe that it is there to wait until the senior person has expressed a view and then agree with it.

Remember that to get a team committed to a plan of action you must encourage it to take part in the planning process. Avoid telling them what they are going to do, like a prophet with tablets of stone.

In the end, however, the team has to get to a plan. The difference between equal voice and equal vote is best shown by an example. In a discussion about where to go on holiday, children have an equal voice – they can say where they want to go – but they certainly don't have a vote.

The account manager's neck is on the block, so in extreme cases he or she may have to use some assertiveness to get to a satisfactory conclusion. In practice there are rarely problems in this area. The team is pleased to be part of the planning process and will normally get amicably to the necessary consensus.

3 *100% agreement:* Allied to the above is the rule of 100% agreement. Read literally, this means that no part of the plan is firm until all members of the team have agreed with it.

It is important. Most planning sessions produce new directions and new activities for all of the members of the team. In many cases these will be in addition to or different from the activities which the team member has underway.

If the momentum of the plan is to be kept up and the new directions implemented, it is vital that everyone agrees and that the timescales and resources have been accurately forecast.

If this rule goes wrong, you will find that people are not disagreeing with a part of the plan only because in fact they have no intention of carrying out their role in it. 'They can write it up if they want, it ain't going to happen.'

4   *Do not duck issues:* Following on the 100% agreement, a successful planning session tables and discusses all the key issues surrounding the plan. Here are some examples of issues that are frequently ducked:

- A person agrees to an activity, but team members do not believe he or she has the necessary knowledge or skills to carry it out.
- A necessary activity is in someone else's province and we duck the issue of how to get that person to buy into the plan.
- An activity is agreed which has a dependency on higher management agreement and no plan is put in place to gain this.
- An activity is agreed which has a dependency on the customer's part and no plan is put in place to ensure that the customer can and does achieve the dependency.

5   *Think before you speak:* Don't stick to this too rigidly because sometimes people do think through an idea while they are articulating it. However, it is a useful rule to agree before the planning session starts so that we can use it to muffle someone who frequently waffles.

The facilitator will present these rules to the team and so long as they agree to abide by them, the planning session proper can begin.

Idea 87 – Connect analysis to objectives tightly

A lot of planning sessions fail because the planners find it impossible to get their brains round a good and detailed analysis and produce objectives that reflect it. You need at this point a neat bridging mechanism to act as a connector between the SWOT analysis and the plan itself. Without this simple device it is very difficult to get a good link, and basically to know where to start.

You need one other ingredient – your critical success factors. What is it that you have to get right to be successful in this account? Write these down in the left column of a matrix with 5 columns. Now number the strengths, weaknesses, opportunities and threats. This is nothing to do with priorities; it is simply a mechanism for identifying each element of the analysis section. In the example, the weaknesses numbered 1,8,9,17 and 23 are the ones the plan will need to eliminate if it is to be strong in CSF 1.

Now under the SWOT headings transfer each item onto the matrix. It will look like this:

Goal area	Remove weaknesses	Exploit opportunities	Avoid threats	Use strengths
Critical success factor 1	1,8,9,17,23	3,4,8,9,14	1,3,4	1,3,4,6,8,12
Critical success factor 2	2,3,7,15,16	1,2,5	2,6,10	2,4,6,8,10,
Critical success factor 3	20,21,22	6,10,11,12	7,8,11	1,3,4,7,8,9
Critical success factor 4	4,5,6,10,11,12	7,13	5,9	2,8,9,12
Critical success factor 5	1,17,24	16		2,7,8,9,11
Critical success factor 6	13,14,18,19,20	15	12,13	13,14
Critical success factor 7	25,27	19,22	14,15	9,11,13
Critical success factor 8	26,28,29	17,18,20,21	16	2,8,12,13

Obey this rule if possible: 'Only allocate a Weakness, Opportunity or Threat to one goal area.' We are getting near allocating responsibility for the achievement of progress in the plan to individuals. Each W, O and T will probably represent a milestone in the activity plan. It is important therefore that no action falls between two people's responsibility – thus the rule.

When it comes to Strengths, we may of course put each Strength into as many goal areas as possible. At action planning time, the team will use the Strengths as pointers to what they can exploit to eliminate Weaknesses.

Idea 88 – Use radar

You get a good view of your strengths and weaknesses if you use a radar diagram to reflect your progress against your critical success factors. As an illustration, here are some common critical success factors for a key customer, along with examples of why you would score yourself as shown:

You get a good view of your strengths and weaknesses if you use a radar diagram to reflect your progress against your critical success factors.

- *CSF 1 – Level of contact – Score 3:* We have never spoken to top management at corporate level. In the division where we are strong we have slumped to a project manager level with the division's general manager meeting us only socially from time to time.
- *CSF 2 – Customer satisfaction – Score 6:* We have performed well and score highly on the customer satisfaction survey. We do not have detailed information of the real benefits our products have given them
- *CSF 3 – Account planning – Score 2:* We have hardly started this and are blocked from getting the process going by our poor level of contact.
- *CSF 4 – Competitive position – Score 8:* It would take a very long time indeed to get rid of our installed base. They are pretty dependent on us
- *CSF 5 – Strategic applications, products and services – Score 6:* We know that what we provide should be strategic, but we do not really know how to exploit this.
- *CSF 6 – Customer strategy – Score 7:* Our knowledge of the customer's strategy gives us confidence that our products and services will continue to be important to them

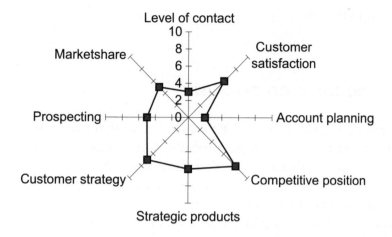

- *CSF 7 – Prospecting – Score 5:* Our pipeline of prospects is not sufficient to reflect our market share. We do not understand the opportunities at corporate or divisional level outside the one division where we are strong
- *CSF 8 – Market share – Score 5:* Our market share has just increased significantly and will continue to do so in the short term as the new projects are implemented. The key to maintaining that momentum is to discover more opportunities in the pipeline.

Idea 89 – Keep the documentation brief

One of the many reasons that people can be put off making creative plans is that they are required to write screeds of data on volumes of forms. The essential part of a plan is simply:

- the list of critical success factors
- the spider's web
- for each objective an activity plan on one page.

The plan should therefore only have about 10 pages, and most people can handle that.

Idea 90 – Become an arsonist?

There is a serious point here. If you sell hardware or anything that can be damaged by fire on your customer's premises, you probably should make sure that the customer has it insured. There is no easier order than the one that comes from, as happened to one of the contributors to this book, replacing three large computer systems catching fire and falling through three floors.

Incidentally, this thought gave rise in the computer industry to a simple test for distinguishing a salesperson from a technical support person. 'What do you do if you are alone in a customer's premises and you see a fire starting in the computer room?' Those whose replies include calling the fire brigade and alerting the customer's duty officer or key holder you make into support people. Those who say 'Go home immediately,' are your salespeople.

The Ten Greatest Sales Tips for Sales Managers

Introduction

Most excellent salespeople end up as sales managers. Here, drawn from the experience of my contributors, are the top tips for when this happens.

Idea 91 – Get the rest of the company to have a healthy perception of the sales force

Many organisations fear their salespeople. They seem to be young for the money they can make and often only come to the attention of the rest of the company if something has gone wrong and, for example, a company is spending time and money trying to deliver a salesperson's promises. Nowadays, it is vital to remove this fear and replace it with a wary respect for the salespeople doing the front line job. There is a cultural point here, with the USA having gone further down the line in this regard than Europe.

Build respect by in the first place dividing the selling job into 'hunting' or 'farming'. Hunting is about bringing in new customers, farming about increasing the amount and type of business you do with your existing customers.

For hunters the main requirement is for persistence and the ability to take knocks. Theirs is the job that has them trying to get interviews with strangers who may not only be unaware of their need but antagonistic to an unsolicited approach whether on the telephone or in person.

Hunters generally work quickly, have short attention spans and feel very dissatisfied if complications of product- or decision-making processes intrude on their getting to the point of closing a sale. They are opportunists and in most cases need watching to make sure that the product being sold is suitable and will work to the promises made by the salesperson.

Some would say that it is the hunters who give salespeople a bad name. There is some truth in that, but they are also the people who make innovation possible and *en masse* bear a lot of responsibility for driving the dollar round in a growth economy.

The hunter is the salesperson who gets a high level of job satisfaction in getting a first order from a new customer. A seller of reprographics expressed it in this way 'You actually have to start by getting yourself invited into the buyer's office. Then you must convince a probable sceptic that what you are offering has benefits over continuing with the people he or she has previously done business with.

'Then you have to find a project, bid for it and win it. The great feeling is that you made it happen, unless you had made the first move and then followed through, that company would have remained loyal to its existing suppliers.'

This is the typical conversation of a hunter. You will recognize some other phrases and sayings in their coffee break chat – 'I thought I'd do one more door'; 'stitched him up in no time flat.'

Many people find the prospect of doing the hunting job horrendous, and organisations are recognising more and more their dependence on such people.

Every salesperson has to have some of the hunter attributes. A good farmer who hates or claims to be bad at new business selling may be too slow to go for the order or not sufficiently assertive to win against the competition. Once again we see the balance that is crucial for a professional account manager, between hustling to get things done and farming for the long term.

Farmers develop skills in long-term relationship building and deep knowledge of a customer's business. A professional sales team selling machine tools, for example, will build over the years a database of customer knowledge that the customer itself may envy. The benefits to a company of professional farmers comes in terms of predictable orders, competitive intelligence, market changes and much more.

In FMCG (fast-moving consumer goods) this knowledge is equally important. The account manager needs to know the detail of the customer's strategy and interface to the consumer.

He or she then needs to know the results of market research and of course of actual sales. The more he or she knows about how the customers sell the product, the more able he or she is to make innovative proposals and achieve stretching sales targets.

Use the hunter/farmer distinction to present your salespeople in the right light, so that the rest of the organisation realises that they have to take the rough parts of what they do along with the smooth parts where they get orders that are easy to deliver.

Idea 92 – Understand the real role of a sales manager

Like it or not, it is the team that produces the results and sales managers at their best are enablers rather than performers.

At some point everyone needs to show that they have thought about their job as a sales manager. Remember KISS – Keep It Simple, Stupid. And get the level right, a mixture of pragmatic efficiency and wide thinking talent reflects the view of the high flier. Here is a question for you – who is responsible for achieving the business results of a sales team? If you answered 'The manager' then you probably need to rethink the relationship between a manager and their team. Like it or not, it is the team that produces the results and sales managers at their best are enablers rather than performers.

Sales managers are there to enable their people to give of their best:

- They are effective implementers of corporate and divisional strategy. They are always able to connect their activities with the bigger picture.
- As well as implementing it, they have a role in influencing high-level strategy. First line managers are the voice of their people, markets and suppliers. They

see the changes day to day and are in the best position to question or suggest alterations to the way the organisation goes about its affairs.

- Managers are a skilled resource to their team. They must add value when they are in action helping the team. When a sales manager goes to see a customer, or a purchasing manager a supplier, for example, the plan must make them do or say something that could not be done or said by the team member. They are the only people who can assure customers that the resources the salesperson is promising will be delivered.

- Sales managers know how the organisation works and can thus add to the efficiency and productivity of their team.

Idea 93 – Don't let your people work too hard

Despite Idea 8 *Remember that no one said life was easy*, if someone gets the work/life balance wrong they will eventually, for whatever reason, sell less or suffer health problems. It is in their and your interest therefore that you interfere and help them to get the balance right. Many managers believe that a salesperson should, after, say, 18 months in a new job, by definition be competent to do it in the contracted hours allowed.

Encourage this type of thinking. As usual your example and leadership will be key to this. People notice, for example, if you have sent them an e-mail at 8 o'clock at night or 6 o'clock in the morning; so you should avoid this.

Idea 94 – Never lose the focus of accountability

Normal account management techniques would say that there should be an account manager for each large customer who may be served through many channels. Plainly the channel manager is responsible for the day-to-day running of their customers, but this should be in the context of an account plan supervised by the account manager.

The account manager needs to prepare this plan and review and update it on a regular basis. It is the planning mechanism that ensures a consistent strategy is presented to the customer across all the channels. The key is to get the right resources at the planning meeting. This will include representatives from marketing as well as the channel managers. This ensures that the strategy is not only consistent for the customer across channels but is also consistent with the organisation's overall plan. It is very useful also to have a senior manager as an account sponsor. Their presence at part, if not all, of the planning meeting gives the account manager the leverage they need to get the resources to implement the plan.

Don't forget the attendance of the customer at this meeting as well. You may bring them in for a presentation of the plan, or even have them there throughout the planning event if both sides get value out of that.

Idea 95 – Show your people the impact of discounting

'Sorry, mate, I've found a cheaper quote.' What does your sales force do when it hears these words? If they generally come straight back to managers asking for permission to give a discount, you have a problem. There is often a simple reason that salespeople do this – they do not understand how a small discount on the sales price produces an inordinately big impact on the bottom line.

Take this example from the insurance industry and transfer it into a real example in your own line of business.

The insurance business has always been price-sensitive. Intermediaries and even consumers who can use the Internet can trawl for the cheapest price. The figures below graphically demonstrate the impact on the bottom line of giving away any of the commission percentage the broker earns from a sale.

Premium	£1000
Cost of insurance	£800
Gross margin	£200
Expenses	£50
Net profit	£150

Here is a sale ruined by discounting commissions. The original commission rate is 20%. This gives the gross margin on £1,000 as £200. Under pressure the salesperson gives a 10% discount. The bottom line has decreased by 66%.

Premium	£900
Cost of insurance	£800
Gross margin	£100
Expenses	£50
Net profit	£50

Idea 96 – Use the rule of 2%

There are many reasons why a reasonable knowledge of the finance side of business is important not only to your sales performance as a sales manager, but also to your career development. Don't be afraid of the detail that this brings you into. Here are two salutary tales of two sales managers with opposing views of how to manage a profit and loss account.

Sally Cranfield is a sales manager at Compusell, a supplier of computer solutions, and she has a problem. Sally's job is to increase sales of computer products and services to her accounts. She has to do it profitably but the important measures she works towards are orders and deliveries, or revenue. This is made more significant by the fact that the salespeople under her are targeted solely on orders. This brings her under huge pressure to make each proposal they put in front of customers as competitive as possible, particularly in terms of price.

Here is the estimated profit and loss account for a deal in which her people are involved.

	No of units	Price per unit	Total
Sales	100	10	1000
Variable costs	100	6	600
Fixed costs			300
Profit			100

The salesperson involved in the sale gives her one problem, production give her another and administration a third. The customer, she is informed by the salesperson, wants to buy from Compusell, but has a cheaper offer from a competitor. He thinks that if Sally could knock just 2% off the price per unit, the purchaser can take a case for buying from Compusell to the board. That discount plus reducing the order to only 98 units will make the customer's budget work.

The production department have had the agreement of management to a slight increase in the price of the unit; it's only 2%, but in the circumstances she cannot pass this on to the customer.

Administration has been saying for some time that there would be a slight increase in their costs due to increased charges from the IT department. It's only 2%.

Sally knows that these four changes to the proposition are all against the interests of her profit and loss account, but the numbers seem small, the customer has a lot of clout, and the salesperson is going to miss his target if he does not get this order. She agrees to the changes.

Look at the actual damage this decision makes to the profit and loss account.

	No of units	Price per unit	Total
Sales	98	9.80	960.40
Variable costs	98	6.12	599.76
Fixed costs			306.00
Profit			54.64

Each 2% adjustment, all to Sally's disadvantage, has combined to knock nearly 46% off the profit of this deal.

Over at HAR, a recruitment consultancy, Andy McRae the new sales director is also taking a number of seemingly small decisions aimed at starting the process of re-establishing falling profitability. One of the products his executives sell is a package of material to clients to keep them up to date on matters to do with employment law.

A major HAR client is likely to buy 100 of these and Andy wonders if the executive could do better. 'I want every one to sell just a few more of these' he says to the executives 'get each client to take just 2% more copies even though we are increasing the selling price a little, by 2%.'

He buys the package from a printer/packager whom he convinces should lower the cost to HAR just a fraction, just 2%.

He had also been working for a while on the administration function and told them to find some economies, 'Every little helps,' he says, 'Just knock me 2% off what you spend right now.'

Andy's starting point was exactly the same as Sally's but he has made the slight adjustments in his favour.

The deal to the major client now looks like this:

	No of units	Price per unit	Total
Sales	102	10.20	1040.40
Variable costs	102	5.88	599.76
Fixed costs			294.00
Profit			146.64

When the 2% works in your favour the addition to the profit is over 46%. Andy's company went from strength to strength – but they never recruited Sally.

When you think that Compusell is doing similar deals all over the world you can see the huge difference these tiny adjustments make. And that is why you need to understand the detail. You will end up making some tough decisions, but the rule of 2% could work for you, starting today.

Idea 97 – Think big as a sales manager and don't look small

Once you have arrived at a certain seniority and trust, you will have considerable freedom to spend the company's money with little chance than the odd misdemeanour will be discovered. Still, don't do it because you could look small to someone: your boss, or your people or at worst your suppliers and customers.

In one of my lecture tours around the USA I was booked by a company to talk to its staff in some twelve cities around the country. Included in these were a number on the East coast. I was therefore somewhat surprised that one of the people who worked for my main sponsor and was based in Boston announced that he was coming to see the event in San Francisco. I assumed that he had to be in San Francisco about that time anyway. How wrong I was. He flew in on the overnight plane and went off to the airport to return to Boston once I had finished the day's work. Subsequently I asked him why, and he said, 'Don't tell anyone, Ken, but I did it for the Frequent Flier Miles. I use them for trips to Europe with my wife.' I suppose it did not matter, but I thought poorly of this. After all, the company does actually pay for Frequent Flier Miles, and this is exactly the sort of budget that gets cut when things are tight. 'Cheapskate,' I thought.

Oh, and if you do get offered First Class on an aeroplane, try it out once by all means; but nowadays Business Class is not far behind and it's half the price.

Idea 98 – Get the compensation strategy for salespeople right

Or suffer the consequences! When a sales compensation or bonus scheme is announced it will normally have been through the hands of many people concerned with giving the sales force the incentives to do what is right for the organisation. They are trying to co-ordinate things so that what is good for the salespeople is also good for the company. Then it is announced and the real experts on compensation get a chance to look at it – the salespeople themselves. If they can find any loophole or flaw that enables them to get benefits without having to work too hard they will find it and exploit it. That is what they are for. So you have to get it right.

All organisations have different ways of doing this, but normally there is a large element of the package that rewards orders with bonuses or commission.

If the sales force is on a straight commission on sales then they are less than 100% motivated to get orders at list price. If you do not reflect the drop in profits caused by discounting in their compensation package, a 10% discount on the sales price has little impact on the salesperson's income but may have reduced bottom line profit by more than 33%. If it is easy to administer, a lot of sales managers use the gross profit of a deal as the basis for sales bonuses, and this works quite well. The other possibility is to discount the sales bonus pro rata to the sales discount, so 90% of list price will yield, say, only 50% of the full sales bonus.

Idea 99 – Survive the budgeting battle

Managers are frequently forced into seeing the annual budgeting round as a battle. I use the term advisedly since the tactics of the people involved obey more of the law of the jungle than the laws of economic good management. They are being asked to predict what is going to happen one year ahead knowing that they will be held responsible for variances to the budget if they get it wrong. And being normal human beings, they do not want to have, or be perceived as having, a lesser job than they had last year.

Managers are frequently forced into seeing the annual budgeting round as a battle.

So much for the owners of the budget. They also have a boss who is looking at the battle from his or her point of view. People who agree budgets with subordinates are keen to be seen by their superiors as taking no nonsense from their people and setting challenging earnings budgets and miserly expenditure budgets.

Here is what both parties do to protect themselves and their dugout:

- Inflate your budget by 10% on the grounds that after a long series of negotiations your boss will pull it back by that amount. This makes everybody happy: you have got the budget you first thought of and your boss can report a hard battle well won.
- Never reveal that there is slack in the budget. If there is one corner of the budget that is set traditionally but does not need to be spent, keep mum. You will have a little pot of gold to put into areas where you actually need to spend money. This is a whole lot easier in the heat of battle than persuading your superiors that there is a real case for increased spending.
- Spend it or lose it. This is a particularly irrational battleground in the war at government department level. If you fail to spend money budgeted for this year,

then next year's budget will be cut by that amount. This leads to remarkable amounts of energy going into chasing suppliers to deliver, on the one hand, and getting the invoice through the system on the other during the last week of the year.

• If you have left it until the last minute, take last year's budget, add inflation, 10% for negotiating slack, see above, and keep the item description as vague as possible. That way you will probably be able to twist and turn during the year to come and come in on target.

All of these tips really have nothing to do with the success of the venture but are reasonable survival techniques. If your boss complains, tell them that nobody said life was fair.

Idea 100 – Avoid the hockey stick approach to sales forecasting

One of the greatest problems sales managers have, and the cause of many an ignominious departure, is getting the sales forecast right.

One of the greatest problems sales managers have, and the cause of many an ignominious departure, is getting the sales forecast right. Too often salespeople get away with the 'hockey stick' approach to forecasting. This shows poor prospects for the next month or quarter but with matters improving enormously over the following periods. If put onto a graph, this looks like an ice hockey stick, pretty flat in the short term and then curving sharply afterwards. Not only that, but they come back during the following period and, guess what, the whole hockey stick has stayed the same shape but simply moved on by one period. Here is a simple process that I have found effective which gives you the opportunity to stop the hockey stick phenomenon.

Divide the prospects into four categories:

- Category A: Those orders which are already in.
- Category B: Those orders which have been agreed by the customer but for which contracts have not been signed or purchase orders raised. Probably 3 out of 4 of these will become orders.
- Category C: Good prospects where there is a good chance of at least half being converted into sales
- Category D: Prospects that can be identified as particular opportunities but which have some way to go before they can be thought likely to happen. Say one in four of these will convert.

Treat each category as follows to get to your best shot at a forecast: 100% of Category A total plus 75% of B plus 50% of C plus 25% of D. While you cannot be sure exactly where the sales revenue will come from, you should have the total sales more or less right.

With three months' practice and experience, salespeople do become more skilled in their sales predictions.